Taylor
Hanby

"I MUSTN'T LET THEM KNOW"

A YANKEE GIRL
AT
FORT SUMTER

BY

ALICE TURNER CURTIS

AUTHOR OF

"The Little Maid" Historical Books
&
"Yankee Girls" Civil War Stories

Illustrated by
ISABEL W. CALEY

APPLEWOOD BOOKS
BEDFORD, MASSACHUSETTS

A Yankee Girl at Fort Sumter was first published by the Penn Publishing Company in 1920. Applewood Books would like to thank Phyllis Butters for lending her copy of *A Yankee Girl at Fort Sumter* for reproduction.

ISBN 1-55709-525-6

Thank you for purchasing an Applewood Book.
Applewood reprints America's lively classics—
books from the past that are still of interest to modern readers.
For a free copy of our current catalog, write to:
Applewood Books, P.O. Box 365, Bedford, MA 01730.

10 9 8 7 6 5 4 3 2 1

Printed and bound in Canada.

Library of Congress Cataloging-in-Publication Data
Curtis, Alice Turner.
    A Yankee girl at Fort Sumter / by Alice Turner Curtis; illus-
trated by Isabel W. Caley.
        p.   cm.
    Summary: When she is caught up in the events that will lead
to the start of the Civil War, ten-year-old Sylvia is glad for the
several good friends, including a young slave girl, she has made
while living in Charleston, South Carolina.
    ISBN 1-55709-525-6
    [1. Charleston (S.C.)—History—Civil War, 1861–1865—Juve-
nile Fiction. 2. Charleston (S.C.)—History—Civil War, 1861–1865
—Fiction. 3. United States—History—Civil War, 1861–1865—
Fiction.]   I. Caley, Isabel W., ill. II. Title
PZ7.C941 Yan   1999
[Fic]—dc21   98-55145
                                            CIP
                                            AC

Introduction

SYLVIA FULTON, a little Boston girl, was staying with her father and mother in the beautiful city of Charleston, South Carolina, just before the opening of the Civil War. She had become deeply attached to her new friends, and their chivalrous kindness toward the little northern girl, as well as Sylvia's perilous adventure in Charleston Harbor, and the amusing efforts of the faithful negro girl to become like her young mistress, all tend to make this story one that every little girl will enjoy reading, and from which she will learn of far-off days and of the high ideals of southern honor and northern courage.

CONTENTS

ILLUSTRATIONS

A Yankee Girl at Fort Sumter

CHAPTER I

SYLVIA

"YOUR name is in a song, isn't it?" said Grace Waite, as she and her new playmate, Sylvia Fulton, walked down the pleasant street on their way to school.

"Is it? Can you sing the song?" questioned Sylvia eagerly, her blue eyes shining at what promised to be such a delightful discovery.

Grace nodded smilingly. She was a year older than Sylvia, nearly eleven years old, and felt that it was quite proper that she should be able to explain to Sylvia more about her name than Sylvia knew herself.

"It is something about 'spelling,'" she explained, and then sang, very softly:

> "'Then to Sylvia let us sing,
>   That Sylvia is spelling.
>   She excels each mortal thing,
>   Upon the dull earth dwelling.'"

"I suppose it means she was the best speller," Grace said soberly.

"I think it is a lovely song," said Sylvia. "I'll tell my mother about it. I am so glad you told me, Grace."

Sylvia Fulton was ten years old, and had lived in Charleston, South Carolina, for the past year. Before that the Fultons had lived in Boston. Grace Waite lived in the house next to the one which Mr. Fulton had hired in the beautiful southern city, and the two little girls had become fast friends. They both attended Miss Patten's school. Usually Grace's black mammy, Esther, escorted them to and from Miss Patten's, but on this morning in early October they were allowed to go by themselves.

As they walked along they could look out across the blue harbor, and see sailing vessels and rowboats coming and going. In the distance were the three forts whose historic names were known to every child in Charleston. Grace never failed to point them out to the little northern girl, and to repeat their names:

"Castle Pinckney," she would say, pointing to the one nearest the city, and then to the long dark forts at the mouth of the harbor, "Fort Sumter, and Fort Moultrie."

"Don't stop to tell me the names of those old forts this morning," said Sylvia. "I know just as much about them now as you do. We shall be late if we don't hurry."

Miss Patten's house stood in a big garden which ran nearly to the water's edge. The schoolroom opened on each side to broad piazzas, and there was always the pleasant fragrance of flowers in the big airy room. Sylvia was sure that no one could be more beautiful than Miss Patten. "She looks just like one of the ladies in your 'Godey's Magazine,'" she had told her mother, on returning home from her first day at school.

And with her pretty soft black curls, her rosy cheeks and pleasant voice, no one could imagine a more desirable teacher than Miss Rosalie Patten. There were just twelve little girls in her school. There were never ten, or fourteen. Miss Patten would never engage to take more than twelve pupils; and the twelve always came. Mrs. Waite, Grace's mother, had told Mrs. Fulton that Sylvia was very fortunate to attend the school.

School had opened the previous week, and Sylvia had begun to feel quite at home with her new schoolmates. The winter before, Mrs. Fulton had taught her little daughter at home; so this was her first term at Miss Patten's.

Miss Patten always stood near the schoolroom door until all her pupils had arrived. As each girl entered the room she made a curtsey to the pretty teacher, and then said "good-morning" to the pupils who had already arrived, and took her seat. When the clock struck nine Miss Rosalie would take her place behind the desk on the platform at the further end of the room, and say a little prayer. Then the pupils were ready for their lessons.

"Isn't Miss Rosalie lovely," Sylvia whispered as she and Grace moved to their seats, "and doesn't she wear pretty clothes?"

Grace nodded. She had been to Miss Rosalie's school for three years, and she wondered a little at Sylvia's admiration for their teacher, although she too thought Miss Patten looked exactly like a fashion plate.

Grace was eager to get to her desk. From where she sat she could see the grim lines of the distant forts; and this morning they had a new value and interest for her; for at breakfast she had heard her father say that, although the forts were occupied by the soldiers of the United States Government, it was only justice that South Carolina should control them, and if the State seceded from the Union Charleston must take possession of the forts. With the consent of the United States Government if possible, but, if this was refused, by force.

Grace had been thinking about this all the morning, wondering if Charleston men would really send off the soldiers in the forts. She had not spoken of this to Sylvia as they came along the street facing the harbor, and now as she looked at the distant forts on guard at the entrance of the harbor, she resolved to ask Miss Rosalie why the United States should interfere with the "Sovereign State of South Carolina," which her father had said would defend its rights. "Question time" was just before the morning session ended. Then each pupil could ask a question. But as a rule only one or two of the girls had any inquiry to make. To-day, however, there were several who had questions to ask, and Grace waited with what patience she could until it was her turn. When Miss Rosalie smiled at her and called her name, Grace rose and said:

"Please, Miss Rosalie, if Charleston owns the forts, could anyone take them away?"

The teacher's dark eyes seemed to grow larger and brighter, and she straightened her slender shoulders as if preparing to defend the rights of her State.

"My dear girl, who would question the right of South Carolina to control all forts on her territory? We all realize that this is a time of uncertainty for our beloved State; we may be treated with harshness, with injustice, but every loyal Carolinian will protect his State."

The little girls looked at each other with startled eyes. What was Miss Rosalie talking about, they wondered, and what did Grace Waite mean about anybody "taking" Fort Sumter or Fort Moultrie? Of course nobody could do such a thing.

School was dismissed with less ceremony than usual that morning, and the little girls started off in groups, talking and questioning each other about what Miss Rosalie had said.

Two or three ran after Grace and Sylvia to ask Grace what she meant by her question.

"Of course we know that northern people want to take our slaves away from us," declared Elinor Mayhew, the oldest girl in school, whose dark eyes and curling hair were greatly admired by auburn-haired, blue-eyed Sylvia, "but of course they can't do that. But how could they take our forts?"

"I don't know," responded Grace. "That's why I asked Miss Rosalie. I guess I'll have to ask my father."

"We'll all ask our fathers," said Elinor, "and to-morrow we will tell each other what they say. I don't suppose *your* father would care if the forts were taken," and she turned suddenly toward Sylvia. "I suppose all the Yankees would like to tell us what we ought to do."

Sylvia looked at her in surprise. The tall girl had never taken any notice of the little Boston girl before, and Sylvia could not understand why Elinor should look at her so scornfully or speak so unkindly. The other girls had stopped talking, and now looked at Sylvia as if wondering what she would say.

"I don't know what you mean," she answered bravely, "but I know one thing: my father would want what was right."

"That's real Yankee talk," said Elinor. "They say slavery isn't right."

There was a little murmur of laughter among the other girls. For in 1860 the people of South Carolina believed they were quite right in buying negroes for slaves, and in selling them when they desired; so these little girls, some of whom already "owned" a colored girl who waited upon them, had no idea but what slavery was a right and natural condition, and were amused at Elinor's words.

"Why do you want to be so hateful, Elinor?" demanded Grace, before Sylvia could reply. "Sylvia has not said or done anything to make you talk to her this way," and Grace linked her arm in Sylvia's, and stood facing the other girls.

"Well, Grace Waite, you can associate with Yankees if you wish to. But my mother says that Miss Patten ought not to have Sylvia Fulton in her school. Come on, girls; Grace Waite can do as she pleases," and Elinor, followed by two or three of the older girls, went scornfully down the street.

"Sylvia! Wait!" and a little girl about Sylvia's age came running down the path. It was Flora Hayes; and, next to Grace Waite, Sylvia liked her the best of any of her new companions.

"Don't mind what Elinor Mayhew says. She's always horrid when she dares to be," said Flora.

Flora's father was a wealthy cotton planter, and their Charleston home was in one of the historic mansions of that city. Beside that there was the big old house on the Ashley River ten miles from the city, where the family stayed a part of the time.

Flora's eyes were as blue as Sylvia's, and her hair was very much the same color. She was always smiling and friendly, and was better liked than Elinor Mayhew, who, as Flora said, was always ready to tease the younger girls.

"I don't know what she meant," said Sylvia as, with Grace on one side and Flora on the other, they started toward home.

"She is just hateful," declared Grace. "I wish I had not asked Miss Rosalie about the forts. But I did want to know. It would be dreadful not to see them where they have always been."

"Oh, Grace! You didn't think they were going to move the forts to Washington, did you?" laughed Flora. "I know better than that. Taking the forts means that the Government of the United States would own them instead of South Carolina."

Grace laughed good-naturedly. She was always as ready to laugh at her own mistakes as at those of others; and in the year that Sylvia had known her she had never seen Grace vexed or angry.

Both Grace and Flora advised Sylvia not to tell her mother of Elinor's unkindness, or of her taunting words. But it was rather difficult for Sylvia to keep a secret from her mother.

"You see, it will make your mother sorry, and she will fret about it," Flora had said; and at this Sylvia had decided that no matter what happened at school she would not tell her mother about it. She almost dreaded seeing Elinor again, and wondered why Elinor's mother had not wanted Miss Patten to take her as a pupil.

Mr. and Mrs. Fulton were surprised when at supper time Sylvia demanded to know what a "Yankee" was. She thought her mother looked a little troubled. But her father smiled. "Yankee is what Britishers call all Americans," he answered.

"Then Elinor Mayhew is just as much a Yankee as I am," thought Sylvia, and she smiled radiantly at the thought that Mrs. Fulton was reassured, and did not question her.

The next day was Saturday, and Mr. Fulton had planned to take his wife and Sylvia to Fort Moultrie. The military band of the fort played every afternoon, and the parapet of the fort was a daily promenade for many Charleston people. During the summer workmen had been making necessary repairs on the fortifications; but visitors were always welcomed by the officers in charge, one of whom, Captain Carleton, was a college friend of Sylvia's father.

Sylvia could row a small boat very well, and her father had purchased a pretty sailboat which he was teaching her to steer. She often went with her father on trips about the harbor, and the little girl always thought that these excursions were the most delightful of pleasures.

There was a favorable breeze this Saturday afternoon, and the little boat, with its shining white paint and snowy sail, skimmed swiftly across the harbor. Sylvia watched the little waves which seemed to dance forward to meet them, looked at the many boats and vessels, and quite forgot Elinor Mayhew's unkindness.

Her mother and father were talking of the black servants, whom they had hired with the house of Mr. Robert Waite, Grace's uncle. Sylvia heard them speak of Aunt Connie, the good-natured black cook, who lived in a cabin behind the Fultons' kitchen.

"Aunt Connie wants to bring her little girl to live with her. Their master is willing, if we have no objections," Sylvia heard her mother say.

"Oh, let the child come," Mr. Fulton responded; "how old is she?"

"Just Sylvia's age. Her name is Estralla," replied Mrs. Fulton.

"You'll have a little darky for a playmate, Sylvia. How will you like that?" her father asked. But before Sylvia could answer, the boat swung alongside the landing-place at the fort and she saw her father's friend, Captain Carleton, waiting to welcome them.

The band was playing, and a few people were on the parapet.

"Not many visitors to-day," said the Captain, as they all walked on together. "I am afraid the

Charleston people resent the fact that the United States is protecting its property."

As they walked along the Captain pointed to the sand which the wind had blown into heaps about the sea-front of the old fort. "A child of ten could easily come into the fort over those sand-banks," he said.

"Whose fort is this?" asked Sylvia, so earnestly that both the Captain and her father smiled.

"It belongs to the United States, of which South Carolina is one," replied the Captain.

Sylvia gave a little sigh of satisfaction. Even Elinor Mayhew could not find any fault with that, she thought, and she was eager to get home and tell Grace what the Captain had said.

On the way back Sylvia asked her mother if she knew that there was a song with her name in it.

"Why, of course, dear child. You were named for that very Sylvia," replied her mother.

> " 'Then to Sylvia let us sing,
>   That Sylvia is excelling;
>   She excels each mortal thing
>   Upon the dull earth dwelling;
>   To her let us garlands bring' "—

sang Mrs. Fulton; "and you can thank your father for choosing your name," she added gaily.

"Oh! But Grace said it was about spelling," explained Sylvia; "but I like your way best," she added quickly.

There were a good many pleasant things for Sylvia to think of that night. Not every girl could be named out of a song, she reflected. Then there was the little colored girl Estralla, who was to arrive the next day, and besides these interesting facts, she had discovered who really owned the forts, and could tell her schoolmates on Monday. All these pleasant happenings made Sylvia forgetful of Elinor Mayhew's unkindness. Before bedtime she had learned the words of the song from which she was named. She knew Grace would think that "excelling" was much better than "spelling."

CHAPTER II

A NEW FRIEND

The next morning Sylvia was awakened by a tapping on her chamber door. Usually Jennie, the colored girl who helped Aunt Connie in the work of the house, would come into the room before Sylvia was awake with a big pitcher of hot water, and Sylvia would open her eyes to see Jennie unfastening the shutters and spreading out the fresh clothes. So this morning she wondered what the tapping meant, and called out: "Come in."

The door opened very slowly and a little negro girl, with a round woolly head and big startled eyes, stood peering in. She was barefooted, and wore a straight garment of faded blue cotton.

For a moment the two children stared at each other. Then Sylvia remembered that Aunt Connie's little girl was coming to live with her mother.

"Are you Estralla?" she asked eagerly, sitting up in bed.

"Yas, Missy," replied the little darky, lifting the big pitcher of water and bringing it into the room, where she stood holding it as if not knowing what to do next.

"Set the pitcher down," said Sylvia.

21

"Yas, Missy," said Estralla, her big eyes fixed on the little white girl in the pretty bed who was smiling at her in so friendly a fashion. She took a step or two forward, her eyes still fixed on Sylvia, and not noticing the little footstool directly in front of her, over which she stumbled with a loud crash, breaking the pitcher and sending the hot water over her bare feet.

"Oh, Mammy! Mammy! Mammy!" she screamed, lying face downward on the floor with the overturned footstool and broken pitcher, while the steaming water soaked through the cotton dress.

In a moment Sylvia was out of bed.

"Get up, Estralla," she commanded, "and stop screaming."

The little darky's wails ceased, and she looked up at the slender white figure standing in front of her.

"I kyan't git up; I'se all scalded and cut," she sobbed, "an' if I does get up I'se gwine to get whipped for breaking the pitcher," and at the thought of new trouble in store for her, she began to scream again.

"Get up this minute," said Sylvia. "I don't believe the water was hot enough to scald you; it never is really hot. Here, help me sop it up," and grabbing her bath towel Sylvia began to mop up the little stream of water which was trickling across the floor.

Estralla managed to get to her feet. She was still holding fast to the handle of the broken pitcher. The front of her cotton dress was soaked, but she was not hurt.

"I'll get whipped, yas'm, I will, fer breaking the pitcher."

"You won't!" declared Sylvia, half angrily. "It's my mother's pitcher, and I'll tell her you didn't mean to break it. Now you go and put on another dress, and tell Jennie to come up here and wipe up this floor."

"I ain't got no other dress; an' if I goes an' tells I'll get whipped," persisted the child.

Sylvia began to wonder what she could do. She thought Estralla was stupid and clumsy to fall down and break the pitcher, and now she thought her silly to be so frightened.

"I tells you, Missy, I su'ly will be whipped," she repeated so earnestly that Sylvia began to believe it. "An' when my mammy sees my dress all wet——" and Estralla began to sob, but so quietly that Sylvia realized the little darky was really frightened and unhappy.

"Don't cry, Estralla," she said more gently, patting her on the shoulder. "I'll tell you what to do. You are just about my size, and I'll give you one of my dresses. It's pink, and it's faded a little, but it's pretty. And you take this towel and wipe up the floor as well as you can. Then you slip off your dress and put on mine." While Sylvia talked Estralla stopped crying and began to look a little more cheerful.

Sylvia ran to the closet and was back in a moment with a pink checked gingham. It had a number of tiny ruffles on the skirt, and a little frill of lace around the neck.

"Landy! You don't mean I kin *keep* that, Missy?" exclaimed Estralla, her face radiant at the very thought.

"Yes, quick. Somebody may come. Slip off your dress."

In a moment the old blue frock lay in a little heap on the floor, and Sylvia had slipped the pink dress over Estralla's head, and was fastening it. The little darky chuckled and laughed now as if she had not a trouble in the world.

"Listen, Estralla! Here, pick up every bit of the pitcher and put the pieces on the chair. Nobody shall know that you broke it. And now you take this wet towel and your dress and spread them somewhere out-doors to dry. You can tell your mammy I gave you the dress. Now, run quick. My mother may come."

Estralla stood quite still looking at Sylvia. She had stopped laughing.

"Will you' mammy scold you 'bout dat pitcher?" she asked.

"I don't know. Anyway, nobody shall know that you broke it. You won't be whipped. Run along," urged Sylvia.

But Estralla did not move. "I don't keer if I is whipped," she announced. "I guess, mebbe, my mammy won't whip hard."

"Sylvia, Sylvia," sounded her mother's voice, and both the little girls looked at each other with startled eyes.

"YOU DON'T MEAN I KIN *KEEP* THAT?"

"Run," said Sylvia, giving Estralla a little push. "Run out on the balcony." Estralla did not question the command, and in a moment, carrying dress and towel, she had vanished through the open window.

"Why, child! What has happened?" exclaimed Mrs. Fulton, coming into the room and looking at the over-turned footstool, the pieces of the broken pitcher, and at Sylvia standing in the middle of the floor with an anxious, half-frightened expression.

"Don't look so frightened, dear child. A broken pitcher isn't worth it," said Mrs. Fulton smilingly. "It's only hot water, and won't hurt anything. Only Father is waiting for breakfast, so use cold water this morning. Here is your blue muslin—I'll tie your sash when you come down," and giving Sylvia a kiss her mother hurried away.

"My landy!" whispered Estralla, peering in from the balcony window. "Your mammy's a angel. An' so is you, Missy. I was gwine tell her the trufe if she'd scolded, I su'ly was. Landy! I'd a sight ruther be whipped than have you scolded, Missy."

Sylvia looked at her in astonishment. Estralla, with round serious eyes, stood gazing at her as if she was ready to do anything that Sylvia could possibly ask.

"Run. It's all right," said Sylvia with a little smile, and Estralla, with a backward look over her shoulder, went slowly out of the room.

"I'm gwine to recollect this jes' as long as I live," Estralla whispered as she made her way back to the kitchen. "Nobuddy ever cared if I was whipped before, or if I wasn't whipped. An' I'll do somethin' fer Missy sometime, I will. An' she give me dis fine dress too." She bent over and smoothed out one of the little ruffles, and chuckled happily.

Her mammy was busy preparing breakfast when Estralla slid quietly into the kitchen. When she did look around and saw the child wearing the pink dress she nearly dropped the dish of hot bacon which Jennie was waiting to take to the dining-room.

"Wha' on earth did you get you' pink dress? Did Missy give it to you? Well, you step out to the cabin and take it off. This minute! Put you' blue frock right on. Like as not her mammy won't let you keep it," and Aunt Connie hurried Jennie off to the dining-room with the breakfast tray.

Estralla did not know what to do. Her blue dress was hung over a syringa bush behind the cabin. And at the dreadful thought that Mrs. Fulton might take away the pink dress she began to cry.

"Missy Sylvia said 'twas faded. She said to put it on," whimpered Estralla.

Aunt Connie began to be more hopeful. If the dress was faded——and she turned and looked at it more closely.

"Well, honey, 'tis faded. An' I guess Missy Sylvia's mammy won' take it back. An' it's the Sabbath day, so you jes' wear it," she said, patting the little woolly head. "Mammy's glad to have you dressed up; but you be mighty keerful."

"Yas, Mammy. I jes' love Missy Sylvia," replied the little girl, now all smiles, and forgetting how nearly she had come to serious trouble.

Nothing more was said to Sylvia about the broken pitcher; but when Jennie put the room in order, and brought down the broken pieces, Aunt Connie exclaimed: "Good massy! It's a good thing my Estralla didn't do that! I'd 'a' cuffed her well, I su'ly would."

Sylvia did not think to tell her mother about the gift of the pink dress to Estralla. She did not feel quite happy that she had not explained the broken pitcher to her mother; but she had promised Estralla that she would not tell, and Sylvia knew that a promise was a very serious thing, something not to be easily forgotten.

She did not see Estralla again that day, and Jennie brought the hot water as usual the next morning.

Grace and Mammy Esther called for Sylvia on Monday morning, and Sylvia at once told her friend that she had been named from the song. This seemed very wonderful to Grace, and she listened to Sylvia's explanation of "excelling" instead of "spelling," and said she didn't think it was of any consequence.

But when Sylvia told her what Captain Carleton had said about the forts, Grace shook her head and looked very serious.

"Don't tell Elinor Mayhew, Sylvia. Because really South Carolina does own the forts. My father said so. He said that South Carolina was a Sovereign State," she concluded.

"What's that? What's a 'sovereign'?" questioned Sylvia.

Grace shook her head. It had sounded like a very fine thing when her father had spoken it, so she had repeated it with great pride.

"We can ask Miss Rosalie," she suggested.

Mammy Esther left the girls at the gate of Miss Patten's garden. As they went up the path Flora Hayes came to meet them.

"I was waiting for you," she said. "I want to ask you both to come out to our plantation next Saturday and spend Sunday. My mother is going to write and ask your mothers if they will give me the pleasure of your company."

"I am sure I can come," declared Grace, "and I think it's lovely of you to ask me."

"You'll come, won't you, Sylvia?" said Flora, putting her arm over the little girl's shoulders as they went up the steps.

"Yes, indeed; thank you very much for asking me," replied Sylvia. She had visited the Hayes plantation early in the summer, and thought it a more wonderful place even than the big mansion on Tradd Street where the Hayes family lived in the winter months. Mr. Hayes owned hundreds of negroes, and raised a great quantity of cotton. The house at the plantation was large, with many balconies, and cool, pleasant rooms. Flora had a pair of white ponies, and there were pigeons, and a number of dogs. Sylvia was sure that it would be a beautiful visit, especially as Grace would be there.

As she went smilingly toward her seat in the schoolroom she passed Elinor Mayhew, who was already seated.

"Yankee!" whispered Elinor sharply, looking at her with scornful eyes.

But Sylvia, remembering that her father had said that all Americans were Yankees, nodded to the older girl and responded: "Yankee yourself!"

CHAPTER III

SYLVIA IN TROUBLE

THE Hayes plantation was about ten miles distant from Charleston, on the opposite side of the Ashley River. Flora told Sylvia and Grace that the Hayes coachman would drive them out, and that they would start early on Saturday morning. Sylvia, remembering her former visit, knew well how delightful the drive would be, and thinking of the pleasure in store quite forgot to be troubled by Elinor Mayhew's hostility.

At recess the girls usually walked about in the garden, or tossed a ball back and forth. Miss Rosalie would sit on the broad piazza overlooking the garden, her fingers busy with some piece of delicate embroidery.

To-day, as they filed out and down the steps, Elinor whispered to several of her companions. And suddenly Sylvia realized that she was standing alone. Grace Waite had lingered to speak to Miss Rosalie; Flora had been excused just before recess, as her black mammy had arrived with a note from Mrs. Hayes. The other girls were gathered in a little group about Elinor, who was evidently telling them something of great interest. Sylvia walked slowly along toward a little summer-house where Miss Patten sometimes had little tea-parties. She hoped Grace would not stay long with Miss Patten. The other girls were between Sylvia and the arbor, and none of them moved to let her pass; nor did any of them speak to her, as she paused with a word of greeting.

"Now, girls," she heard Elinor say; and the others, half under their breath, but only too distinctly for Sylvia, called out: "Yankee, Yankee!" Then like a flock of bright-colored birds they ran swiftly into the summer-house.

For a moment Sylvia stood quite still. She realized that Elinor meant to be hateful; but she remembered that her father had said that all Americans were called "Yankees," and she was not a coward. She went straight on to the arbor. Elinor Mayhew stood on the steps.

"You are just as much a Yankee as I am. And you ought to be proud of it," declared Sylvia, facing the older girl.

"Hear that, girls!" called Elinor to the group about her. There was a little angry murmur from the others.

"Don't you dare say that again, Miss Boston," called May Bailey, who stood next to Elinor.

Sylvia was now thoroughly angry. She knew of no reason why these girls should treat her in so unkind a fashion. She felt very desolate and unhappy, but she faced them bravely.

"Yankees! Yankees! It's what all Americans are," she declared defiantly.

In an instant the little girls were all about her. Elinor Mayhew was holding her hands, and the others were pushing her along the path to the shore. The thick growing shrubs hid them from the house. Sylvia did not cry out or speak. She was not at all afraid, nor did she resist.

"We ought to make her take it back," said May Bailey, as Elinor stopped, and they all stood in a close group about Sylvia.

"Of course she's got to take it back, and apologize on her knees," declared Elinor. "She might as well learn that South Carolinians will not be insulted," and Elinor lifted her head proudly.

"I won't take it back!" retorted Sylvia, "and you are the ones who will have to apologize. Yes, every one of you, before I will ever speak to you again."

"Hear that, girls! Wouldn't it be dreadful if she never spoke to us again!" sneered Elinor.

"She means she will tell Miss Rosalie," said one of the girls.

"I don't, either. I can look after my own affairs," retorted Sylvia bravely. "I'm not a telltale. Although I suppose girls who act the way you do would tell."

"Get down on your knees," commanded Elinor, trying to push the little girl.

"There's the bell," and they all turned and scampered back to the house, leaving Sylvia on the path; for Elinor had let go of her so suddenly that she had fallen forward.

Her knees were hurt, and one of her hands was bruised by the fall. For a moment she lay sobbing quietly. She was angry and miserable. She had been brave enough when the girls had seemed to threaten her, but now her courage was gone. She could not go back to the schoolroom and face all those enemies. If Miss Rosalie came in search of her she might not be able to resist telling her what had happened; and, miserable and unhappy as she was, Sylvia resolved that she would never tell.

"But Elinor Mayhew and all the rest of them shall be sorry for this. Yes, they shall," she sobbed as she got to her feet and turned toward the shore. She knew she must either go straight back to the schoolroom or else find a hiding-place until they had ceased to search for her. There was a wall at the foot of the garden, covered with fragrant jessamine and myrtle. If she could only get over that wall, thought Sylvia, she would be safe. She ran swiftly forward and began to scramble up, grasping the sturdy vines, and finding a foothold on some bit of rough brick. She reached the top just as she heard Miss Rosalie's servant calling her name.

Sylvia looked down to the further side. The vines drooped over and below the wall a high bank of sand sloped to the shore. Holding tight to the vines she slid down, hitting her bruised knees against the rough surface. The vines cut her hands, and when she tumbled into the sand her dress was torn and soiled, her pretty hair-ribbon was gone, and her once white stockings were grimy. Beside these misfortunes her hands were bleeding.

Never in all her life had Sylvia been so wretched. She sat quite still in the warm sand, and wondered what she could do. If she went home her mother would insist upon an explanation of her untidy condition. Beside that Sylvia was not sure if she could find her way home unless she climbed back into the garden. She looked along the shore at the landing-place not far distant where several boats were bobbing up and down in the wash of the incoming tide. She could see boats coming and going between the forts and the city. She could see grim Fort Sumter, with its guns that seemed to look straight at her. She watched a schooner coming across the bay, and realized that it was coming to that very wharf. A number of men landed, and several carts came down and boxes were unloaded, and negroes carried them to the schooner.

Sylvia got up and walked along the shore until she was near the wharf, and stood watching the negroes as they lifted the heavy boxes. She wished she could ask one of them to tell her the way home. Then she noticed a tall figure in uniform coming up the wharf.

"It's Captain Carleton!" she exclaimed joyfully, quite forgetting for the moment her torn dress and scratched hands as she ran toward him.

"Why! Is it Sylvia Fulton?" exclaimed the surprised Captain, looking down at the untidy little figure. "Why, what has happened?"

"Oh, dear," sobbed Sylvia, "I guess I'm lost."

"Well, well! It's lucky you came down to this wharf. Come on board the schooner, and we'll see to these little hands first thing," and the good-natured Captain rested a kindly hand on the little girl's shoulder and walked down the wharf. Sylvia heard the men talking of the Charleston Arsenal, and of the boxes of arms which were to be taken on the schooner to Fort Sumter.

The Captain bathed the little hurt hands and flushed face, talking pleasantly to the little girl about the schooner, and asking her if she did not think it a much finer craft than her father's small boat; so in a little while she was comforted and quite at home.

"Now, sit here by the cabin window, and I will come back and take you home as soon as I settle this trouble about my supplies," and the Captain hurried back to the wharf.

Sylvia sat quite still and looked out of the round porthole. She felt very tired, and leaned her head against the cushioned wall. She could hear the monotonous chant of the negroes, and feel the swaying motion of the vessel, and soon was fast asleep. She did not know when the schooner was towed out into the channel, nor when the sails were hoisted and they went sailing down the bay.

For Captain Carleton had entirely forgotten his little guest. When he hurried back to the wharf he discovered a little group of Charleston citizens, one of whom was Elinor Mayhew's father, disputing the right of the United States officers to take guns from the Charleston Arsenal to Fort Sumter; and when the matter was settled he had hurried the departure of the vessel. Not until they were ready to land at the fort did he remember his little friend. He went down to the cabin, and found Sylvia fast asleep.

"Poor little Yankee! I wonder what will happen to her if South Carolina really leaves the Union," he thought, and then his face grew troubled as he remembered that Mr. and Mrs. Fulton must be in great trouble and anxiety over the disappearance of their little daughter. But first of all he must see the schooner's cargo safely unloaded at Fort Sumter, and send his men back to Fort Moultrie; then he would take Sylvia home, or find some way to notify her parents that she was safe and well cared for.

CHAPTER IV

AN UNEXPECTED JOURNEY

WHEN Sylvia did not come in with the other girls Miss Patten sent a maid in search of her. But she did not search very carefully. She called Sylvia's name a few times, sauntered about the garden, and then reported: "Can't find Missy Sylvia."

She was then told to go straight to Mrs. Fulton's house on the East Battery and see if Miss Sylvia had reached home. Miss Patten did not feel anxious. She thought it probable that the little northern girl did not realize the rules of the school, had become tired, and so started for home.

"Did Miss Sylvia say anything to any of you young ladies about leaving the grounds?" she questioned the pupils. But they all declared that they knew nothing of her whereabouts.

"She was on the path behind us when the bell rang, volunteered May Bailey.

Elinor's face was unusually flushed, and she kept her eyes on her book. Probably the "little Yankee," as she called Sylvia even in her thoughts, had run home to tell her mother of the trouble.

By the time Miss Patten's messenger had reached the Fulton house Sylvia was in the cabin of the little schooner. The girl gave her message to Mrs. Fulton in so indefinite a manner that at first Sylvia's mother hardly understood whether Sylvia was in the garden of the school, or had started for home. Estralla was standing near the steps and began whimpering: "Oh, Missy Sylvia los'! That w'at she say. She lost!"

"Nonsense, Estralla! Sylvia could not be lost in Miss Patten's garden," said Mrs. Fulton; but she decided to return to the school with the maid.

As they went down the street Estralla followed close behind. Her bare feet made no noise, but now and then she choked back a despairing little wail. For the little colored girl was sure that some harm had befallen her new friend.

When Mrs. Fulton appeared at the schoolroom door Miss Patten was greatly alarmed. Elinor Mayhew and May Bailey exchanged a look of surprised apprehension. They felt sure that Sylvia had hurried home and told her mother just what had happened. If she had, and Mrs. Fulton had come to inform Miss Patten, they knew there would be unpleasant things in store for them.

In a short time a thorough search for the lost girl was in progress. Servants were sent along the streets, and Mrs. Fulton hastened home thinking it possible that Sylvia might be in her own room.

No one paid any attention to the little colored girl in the faded blue cotton gown who wandered about the paths and around the summer-house. Estralla noticed two of the older girls talking together, and heard the taller one say: "Well, wherever she is, she needn't think we will ever take back one word. She *is* a Yankee!"

"They'se done somethin' to my missy," decided Estralla. "They'se scairt her." She ran down the path toward the wall at the end of the garden, and stopped suddenly; for right in front of her, caught on the jessamine vine which grew over the wall, she saw a fluttering blue ribbon. "Dat's off'n Missy Sylvia's hair, dat ribbon is," she whispered, reaching up for it. Holding it fast in her hands she looked closely at the mass of heavy vines, and nodded her little woolly head. "Dat's w'at she done. She clumb right up here, to git away frum those imps o' Satan w'at was a plaguein' her," decided Estralla, and in an instant she was going up the wall in a much easier manner than had been possible for Sylvia. She dropped on the further side, just as Sylvia had done, and traced Sylvia's steps to near the landing-place. Then she stopped short. Men were loading boxes on a schooner at the end of the pier, and she could see a tall officer in uniform standing on the deck of the vessel.

"Hullo, here's another small girl. Black one this time," said one of the white sailors.

"Yas, Massa! Please whar' is my missy?" replied the little darky eagerly.

"Safe in the cabin," nodded the good-natured man.

Estralla slipped behind a pile of boxes, and watched for a chance to get on board the vessel without being seen. She had heard many tales, told by the older colored people, of little children, yes, and grown people, too, who had been enticed on board vessels in far-off African ports, and carried off to be sold into slavery. Estralla remembered that all those people in the stories were black; but who could tell but what there was some place in the world where white people were sold? Anyway, she resolved that wherever Missy Sylvia went she would go with her.

In a few moments she saw a chance to run over the gangplank. She went straight toward the cabin door and peered in. Yes, there was Missy Sylvia on the broad cushioned seat under the window. Very softly Estralla tiptoed across the cabin. Just as she was about to speak Sylvia's name the sound of approaching footsteps startled her, and, sure that she would be sent on shore by whoever might discover her, she looked about for a hiding-place, and the next instant she was curled up under the very seat on which Sylvia was asleep.

It was not long before Estralla followed her missy's example. But she was wide awake when Captain Carleton came into the cabin.

As soon as he returned to the deck Estralla crawled out from her hiding-place and looked about her.

"Wake up, Missy," she whispered leaning over Sylvia; and Sylvia sat up quickly, with a little cry of astonishment.

"Don't you be skeered," said Estralla softly, "'cause I ain' gwine to let you be carried off. I knows jes' how slaves are ketched. Yas'm, I does. My mammy tole me. They gits folks in ships and carries 'em off an' sells 'em to folks. An' I ain' gwine to let 'em have you, Missy." There were tears in Estralla's eyes. She knew that her own brother had been sold the previous year and taken to a plantation in Florida. She had heard her mother say that she, Estralla, might be sold any time. She knew that slavery was a dreadful thing.

"Where are they taking us?" questioned Sylvia, for she realized that the vessel was moving swiftly through the water. She wondered why Captain Carleton had gone away. Seeing Estralla there gave her a dreadful certainty that what the little darky said might be true. Perhaps the vessel might have others on board who were being taken off to be sold, as Estralla declared.

"Yas, Missy. My mammy's tole me jes' how white folks gets black folks fer slaves. Takes 'em away from their mammies, an' never lets 'em go back. Yas!" And Estralla's big eyes grew round with terror.

"But I am a white girl, Estralla," said Sylvia.

Estralla shook her head dolefully.

"Yas, Missy. But I'se gwine to git you safe home. You do jes' as I tell you an' you'll be safe back with your mammy by ter-morrow!" she declared.

"You lay down and keep your eyes tight shut till I comes back," she added, and Sylvia, tired and frightened, obeyed.

The schooner was now coming to her landing at Fort Sumter. Estralla managed to get on deck without being noticed. She did not know where they were, but wherever it was she resolved to get Sylvia out of the vessel, and ran back to the cabin.

"Now, don' you speak to nobuddy. Jes' keep right close to me," she whispered. And Sylvia obeyed. The two little girls crept up the cabin stairs, and crouching close to the side of the cabin made their way toward the stern of the vessel.

The crew and the soldiers and Captain Carleton were now all toward the bow. A small boat swung at the stern of the schooner.

"Now, Missy, we's got to git ourselves into that boat and row back home," whispered Estralla, grasping the rope.

At that moment Sylvia turned to look back. She could see a tall officer on the forward deck, and without an instant's hesitation she ran toward him calling:

"Captain Carleton! Captain Carleton!" He turned smilingly toward her, and Sylvia clasped his hand.

"I didn't know where I was," she said.

"You are at Fort Sumter. And it's all my fault," he answered. "I forgot all about you until we were nearly here. But one of my men is going to sail you safely home. What's this?" he added, as Estralla appeared by Sylvia's side.

"It's Estralla. Her mammy is our cook," said Sylvia.

The Captain looked a little puzzled. He wondered how the little darky had got on board the vessel without being seen.

"Well, she will be company for you. And you must ask your father and mother to forgive my carelessness in taking you so far from home," said the Captain.

It was sunset when Sylvia and Estralla, escorted by one of the soldiers from Fort Sumter, came walking up East Battery. Mrs. Fulton was on the piazza, and Mrs. Waite and Grace were with her. Grace was the first to see and recognize Sylvia, and with a cry of delight ran to welcome her.

The soldier had a note for Mrs. Fulton explaining that Sylvia, apparently on her way from school, had wandered down to the landing, and of Captain Carleton's forgetting her presence in the cabin, so that Sylvia was not questioned that night in regard to her disappearance from Miss Patten's. Grace knew nothing of Sylvia's encounter with Elinor Mayhew, so no one could imagine why she had started for home without a word to Miss Patten.

Mrs. Fulton was too rejoiced to have her little girl safely at home to question or blame her.

Sylvia was not hungry. The officer in charge of Fort Sumter had given the two children an excellent supper. But she was tired and very glad to have a warm bath and go straight to bed.

"Oh, Mother! This has been the most horrid day in all my life," she said, as her mother brushed out the tangled yellow hair, and helped her prepare for bed.

"It has been rather hard for your father and me," Mrs. Fulton reminded her; "we began to fear some dreadful thing had happened to our little girl. Promise me, Sylvia, never to run away from school again."

Sylvia promised. She wished she could tell her mother that it was not school she ran away from; that she was trying to escape the taunts and unfriendliness of her schoolmates. But she remembered her promise. She had declared proudly that she should not tell, and hard as it was she resolved that she would keep that promise. But she wished with all her heart that she need not go to school another day.

"Do I have to go to Miss Patten's school, Mother?" she asked in so unhappy a voice that Mrs. Fulton realized something unpleasant had happened.

"We will talk it over to-morrow, dear," she said; "go to sleep now," and Sylvia crept into the white bed quite ready to sleep, but wondering how she could talk about going to school, and still keep her promise, when to-morrow came.

CHAPTER V

ESTRALLA AND ELINOR

In the morning Sylvia did not refer to what had happened the day before, so her mother decided not to question her. Grace and Flora both arrived at an early hour to accompany Sylvia to school. They were eager to hear how she had happened to be on the schooner which had carried arms to Fort Sumter from the Charleston Arsenal. But Sylvia did not seem to want to talk of her adventure, and both the little southern girls were too polite to question her.

"Father says those guns don't belong to the United States, they belong to South Carolina."

Sylvia did not reply. She recalled one of her lessons, however, where she had learned that the United States meant each and every State in the Union and she remembered what Captain Carleton had said.

"Mother says I may go with you on Saturday, Flora," interrupted Grace; "I wish it was Friday this minute."

"So do I," agreed Flora laughingly; "and we must teach Sylvia to ride on one of the ponies this time."

For on the previous visit Sylvia had said that she wished she could ride as Flora did.

"Oh! Truly? Flora, do you really mean it?" Sylvia asked.

"Of course I do. We will have a ride Saturday afternoon and again Sunday," replied Flora.

With the pleasure of the plantation visit in store Sylvia for the moment forgot all about her dread of facing the girls at school. Miss Patten detained her at the door of the schoolroom with a warmer greeting than usual, but said: "My dear, I want to talk with you at recess;" but her smile was so friendly and her words so kind that Sylvia was not troubled. As she passed Elinor's seat she did not look up, but the whisper, "Yankee," made her flush, and brought back all her dislike of the tall, handsome Elinor.

At recess, after the other girls had left the schoolroom, Miss Patten came to Sylvia's desk and sat down beside her.

"Sylvia, dear," she said gently, "I want you to tell me why you started off alone yesterday. Had anything happened here at school to make you so unhappy that you did not want to stay?"

Sylvia looked up in surprise. Why, Miss Patten seemed to know all about it, she thought. How easy it would be to tell her the whole story. But suddenly she resolved that no matter what Miss Patten knew, she, Sylvia, must not break her word. So she looked down at her desk, and made no reply.

"I am sure none of the other pupils would mean to hurt your feelings, Sylvia. But if any of them have carelessly said something that sounded unkind, I know they will apologize," continued the friendly voice; and again Sylvia looked up. If she told what Elinor and May had said she was now sure that Miss Rosalie would make them both say they were sorry; and Sylvia remembered that she had declared to them that they should do exactly that.

"Would they really, Miss Patten?" she asked in so serious a voice that the teacher believed for the moment that she would soon know the exact reason why Sylvia had fled from the school; and she was right, she was about to hear it, but not from Sylvia.

There was a little silence in the quiet pleasant room where the scent of jessamine and honeysuckle came through the open windows, and no sound disturbed the two at Sylvia's desk. Sylvia was assuring herself that she really ought to tell Miss Patten; but somehow she could not speak. If she broke a promise, even to an enemy, as she felt Elinor Mayhew to be, she would despise herself. But Elinor would have to apologize for the way she had treated Sylvia. Just at this moment of hesitation a round woolly head appeared at one of the open windows. Two small black hands rested on the window-sill, and a moment later Estralla, in her faded blue dress, was standing directly in front of Miss Patten and Sylvia.

"I begs pardon, Missy Teacher. But I knows my missy ain't done nuffin' to be kept shut up for. An' I knows why she runned off yesterd'y. Yas'm. I heered dat tall dark girl an' nuther girl sayin' as how Missy Sylvia was a Yankee. Yas'm; and as how they was glad they called her names. Yas'm, I sho' heered 'em say those very words," and Estralla bobbed her head, and stood trembling in every limb before "Missy Teacher," not knowing what would happen to her, but determined that the little white girl, who had protected her, and given her the fine pink dress, should not be punished.

"Oh, Estralla!" whispered Sylvia, her face brightening.

Miss Rosalie stood up, and rested her hand on Sylvia's shoulder.

"And so you would not tell, or complain about your schoolmates?" Then without waiting for a reply, she leaned over and kissed Sylvia. "That is right, dear child. I am proud to have you as a pupil. Now," and she turned to Estralla, "you run home as fast as you can go. Your young mistress is not being punished, and will not be. But you did just right in coming to tell me. But the next time you come remember to come in at the door!" and Miss Rosalie smiled pleasantly at the little darky, whose face now was radiant with delight.

"Yas'm. I sho' will 'member," and with a smile at Sylvia, Estralla tiptoed toward the open door and disappeared.

It was a very grave teacher who watched her pupils return to their seats that morning. It was a time when all the people in the southern city were anxious and troubled. There had always been slaves in South Carolina, and now the Government of the United States was realizing that the black people must not be kept in servitude; that they had the same rights as white people; and it was difficult for the Charleston people to acknowledge that this was right.

Miss Rosalie was a South Carolinian, and she was sure that Charleston people did right to insist on keeping their slaves, even if it meant war. And it now seemed likely that the North and South might come to warfare. The word "Yankee" was as hateful to Miss Rosalie as it was to Elinor Mayhew, and for that very reason she determined that Elinor should make a public apology for calling one of her schoolmates a "Yankee." To the Carolinians the name meant the name of their enemies, and it seemed to Miss Rosalie a very dreadful thing to accuse this little northern girl of being an enemy.

After the girls were all seated she said in a very quiet tone:

"Elinor, please come to the platform."

For a moment Elinor hesitated. Then she walked slowly down the aisle and stood beside Miss Patten.

"Now, young ladies, I do not need to explain to you the meaning of the word 'courtesy.' You all know that it means kindness and consideration of the rights and feelings of others. You know as well the meaning of the word 'hospitality'; that it means that any person who is received beneath your roof is entitled to courtesy and to more than that, to protection. Even savages will protect any traveler who comes into their home, and give the best they have to make him comfortable." Miss Rosalie stopped a moment, and then said: "If there is anyone of you who has not known the meaning of the two words to which I refer, will she please to rise."

The girls all remained seated.

"Elinor, you will now apologize for having failed in courtesy and in hospitality to one of my pupils."

Elinor stood looking out across the schoolroom. Her mouth was tightly closed, and apparently she had no intention of obeying.

"Do I have to apologize for speaking the truth?" she demanded.

The girls held their breath. Was it possible that Elinor dared defy Miss Patten? Grace and Flora were sadly puzzled. They were the only pupils who did not understand the exact reason, Elinor's treatment of Sylvia, for Miss Patten's demand.

The teacher did not respond, and Elinor did not speak. Then after a moment Miss Patten said, "Take your seat, Elinor. I shall make this request of you again at the beginning of the afternoon session. If you do not comply with it you will no longer be received as a pupil in this school."

CHAPTER VI

SYLVIA AT THE PLANTATION

WHEN the afternoon session opened Elinor Mayhew was not in her usual place. Grace and Flora had been told by the other girls what had happened on the day of Sylvia's disappearance from school. May Bailey had declared that Sylvia must have "run straight to the teacher," and that she was a telltale as well as a "Yankee." Grace had defended her friend warmly.

"I don't know how Miss Rosalie found out, but I'm sure Sylvia did not tell," she declared.

Flora was unusually quiet. There were many scornful looks sent in Sylvia's direction that afternoon, which Miss Patten noticed and easily understood. Before school was dismissed she said that she had a brief announcement to make.

"I want to say to you that the pupil whom Elinor treated with such a lack of courtesy did not inform me of the fact. Nor would she say one word against any of her schoolmates when I questioned her. Someone who overheard Elinor's unfriendly remarks came and told me."

Flora Hayes smiled and drew a long breath. She did not blame Sylvia for being a "Yankee," but it had troubled her to think of her new friend as a "telltale," whatever her provocation might have been. The other girls began to look at Sylvia with more friendly eyes, and as they ran down the steps several found a chance to nod and smile at her, or to exchange some word. So Sylvia began to feel that her troubles were over, if Elinor Mayhew did not return to school.

"Father, are you sure 'Yankee' doesn't mean anything beside 'American'?" she asked in a very serious tone, as she sat beside Mr. Fulton on the piazza that evening. They were quite alone, as Mrs. Fulton had stepped to the kitchen to speak to Aunt Connie.

"The girls at school all think it means something dreadful," she added.

"Let me see, Sylvia. You study history, don't you?" responded her father slowly. "Of course you do; and you know that George Washington and General Putnam and General Warren, and many more brave men, defended this country and its liberty?"

"Why, yes," replied Sylvia, greatly puzzled.

"The men of South Carolina were among the bravest and most loyal of the defenders of our liberties. And when America's enemies called American men 'Yankees' they meant General Washington and every other American who was ready to defend the United States of America. So if any of your friends use the word 'Yankee' scornfully they agree with the enemies of the Union. No one need be ashamed of being called a 'Yankee.' It means someone who is ready to fight for what is right."

But Sylvia still wondered. "The girls don't think so," she said.

"Well, that is because they don't understand. They will know when they are older," said Mr. Fulton. He did not imagine that any of the companions of his little daughter had treated her in an unfriendly fashion, and thought it a good opportunity to make her understand the real meaning of the word.

"You are a Yankee girl. And that means you must always try to protect other people who need protection," said her father.

Sylvia's face brightened. She could easily understand that. It meant that she must not let Estralla get a whipping when she had not deserved it; and she was glad she had not told the real story of the broken pitcher. She resolved always to remember what her father had said.

The remainder of the week passed pleasantly. Elinor Mayhew did not return to school, and the other girls profited by her example and no longer teased or taunted the little northern girl.

Saturday morning proved to be perfect weather for the drive to the Hayes plantation. The sun shone, the clear October air was full of autumnal fragrance, and when the Hayes carry-all, drawn by two pretty brown horses, and driven by black Chris, the Hayes coachman, and Flora's black mammy on the seat beside him, stopped in front of Sylvia's house and Flora came running up the path, Sylvia and Grace were on the steps all ready to start.

There was plenty of room for all three girls on the back seat, and Flora declared that Sylvia should sit between Grace and herself. Mrs. Fulton and Estralla stood at the gate and watched the happy little party drive off. Estralla looked very sober. Ever since the adventure at Fort Sumter the little colored girl had felt that she must look after Missy Sylvia carefully. And she was not well pleased to see her young mistress disappear from her watchful eyes.

"What a funny name 'Estralla' is," laughed Flora, as Sylvia called back a good-bye.

"Oh, that isn't her name, really," explained Grace. "You know my Uncle Robert owns her, and Auntie Connie named her after Aunt Esther and Cousin Alice. Her name is really Esther Alice. But the colored people never speak as we do."

"How can anybody 'own' anybody else, even if their skin is black?" asked Sylvia.

Both her companions looked at her in such evident surprise that Sylvia was sure she ought not to have asked such a question. Suddenly she remembered that Flora's "Mammy" and "Uncle Chris," as Flora called him, were negroes, and of course must have heard. She resolved not to ask another question during her visit.

Their way took them through pleasant streets shaded by spice trees and an occasional oak. From behind high walls came the fragrance of orange blossoms, ripening pomegranates and grapes. Very soon they had crossed the Ashley River, and now the road ran between broad fields of cotton where negroes were already at work gathering the white fluffy crop which would be packed in bags and bales and shipped to many far distant ports.

The three little friends talked gaily of the pleasant visit which had just begun. Sylvia was hoping that Flora would again speak of the promised ride on one of the white ponies, but not until Uncle Chris guided the swift horses into the driveway, shaded by fine live-oaks, which led to the big house, was her wish gratified.

"We'll have a ride this afternoon, girls, if you are not too tired," she said.

Grace and Sylvia promptly declared that they were not at all tired, and that a ride was just what they would like best.

The plantation's "big house," as the negroes called the owner's home, was the largest house Sylvia had ever entered. Its high piazza with the tall pillars was covered by a tangle of jessamine vines and climbing roses. The front hall led straight through the house to another piazza, which looked out over beautiful gardens and a tiny lake. Behind a thick hedge of privet were the cabins of the house servants. The negroes who did the work on the plantation, caring for the horses and cows, and working in the cotton fields, lived at some distance from the "big" house.

Mrs. Hayes came out on the piazza to welcome the party. She had come down from Charleston on the previous day. It seemed to Sylvia she had never seen so many negroes before in all her life. Neat colored maids were flitting about the house, colored men were at work in the garden, and colored children peered smilingly around the corner of the house.

A colored maid was told to look after Grace and Sylvia, and she led the way up the beautiful spiral staircase to a pleasant chamber overlooking the garden. There were two small white beds, with a little mahogany light-stand between them. On this stand stood a tall brass candle-stick. There were two dressing tables, and two small bureaus, and a number of comfortable chintz-covered chairs. The floor was of dark, shining wood, and beside each bed was a long, soft white rug.

Sylvia and Grace knew that this room had been arranged especially for any of Flora's young friends whom she might entertain, and they both thought it was one of the nicest rooms that anyone could imagine. The smiling colored maid brushed their hair, helped them into the fresh muslin dresses they had each brought, and when they were ready opened the door and followed them down the stairs where they found Flora awaiting them.

"Luncheon is all ready," she said, and led the way into the dining-room, where Mrs. Hayes and Flora's two older brothers, Ralph and Philip, were waiting for them. The boys were tall, good-looking lads, and as they were in the uniform of the Military School of Charleston, of which they were pupils, Sylvia thought they must be quite grown up, although Ralph was only sixteen and his brother two years younger. They had ridden out on horseback from Charleston, and had just arrived.

Flora introduced them to Sylvia, and Grace greeted them as old acquaintances.

"I suppose you girls are looking forward to the corn-shucking to-night?" Ralph asked, with his pleasant smile, as he held Sylvia's chair for her to take her seat at the table, while Philip performed the same service for Grace.

"Oh, my dear boy! You have betrayed Flora's surprise," said Mrs. Hayes. "She had planned not to let the girls know about it until nightfall."

"What is a 'corn-shucking'?" questioned Sylvia; for she had always lived in a city and did not know much about farm or plantation affairs.

"Shall I tell her, Flora?" questioned Ralph, laughingly.

"No! No, indeed! Wait, Sylvia, then it will be a surprise after all," responded Flora.

Sylvia smiled happily. She was sure that this visit was going to be even more delightful than when she had been Flora's guest in the early spring. There seemed to be so many things to do on a plantation, she thought.

The young people were all hungry, and enjoyed the roasted duck, with the sweet-potatoes and the grape jelly. Beside these there were hot biscuit and delicious custards. Sylvia had finished her custard when two maids brought a large tray into the room, and in a moment the little girls exclaimed in admiring delight; for the tray contained two doves, made of blanc-mange, resting in a nest of fine, gold-colored shreds of candied orange-peel, and an iced cake in the shape of a fort, with the palmetto flag on a tiny staff.

At the sight of their State flag both the boys arose from their seats and saluted.

"That's the flag to fly over Charleston's forts!" declared Ralph as he sat down.

After luncheon was over Mrs. Hayes advised the girls to lie down for a little rest before starting for their ride. But they all declared they were not tired, and there were so many things to see and enjoy at the plantation that Sylvia and Grace were delighted when Flora suggested that first of all they should go out through the garden to the negro quarters, stopping at the stables on their way for a look at the ponies.

Sylvia was ready before the other girls and stood on the piazza waiting. She was leaning against one of the vine-covered pillars that supported the piazza, and

Ralph and Philip, who were sitting just around the corner, did not know she was there and could not see her. Sylvia could hear their voices, but did not at first notice what they were saying until the word" Yankee" caught her ear.

"The first thing you know those northern Yankees will take our forts," she heard Philip say, and heard Ralph laugh scornfully as he responded: "They can't do it, or free our slaves, either. Say, did you know Father was going to sell Dinkie; she's making such a fuss that I reckon she'll get a lashing; says she don't want to leave her children."

There was a little silence, and then the younger boy spoke.

"I wish they wouldn't sell Dinkie. I hate to have her go. It isn't fair. Of course she feels bad to leave those little darkies of hers. Jove!" and the boy's voice had an angry tone, "Dinkie shan't be whipped! I won't have it. She used to be my mammy."

Suddenly Sylvia realized that she was listening, and ran down the steps toward the little lake which lay glimmering in the sun beneath the shade of the overhanging pepper trees. She ran on past the lake down a little path which led toward the pine woods. She no longer felt happy, and full of anticipations of the surprise in store at the corn-shucking. All she could think of was "Dinkie," a woman who was to be sold away from her children, and who was to be whipped because she rebelled against the cruelty of her master.

"It's because she's a slave," Sylvia whispered to herself. "I hate slavery. My father said Yankees always fought for what was right. Why don't they fight against slavery?" She quite forgot that Flora and Grace world wonder where she had gone, and be alarmed at her absence.

"I do wish I could see Dinkie," she thought. "I wish I could do something to help set every slave free." Then she remembered that Philip had declared that Dinkie should neither be sold nor whipped.

"I like Philip," she declared aloud, and was surprised to hear a little chuckling laugh from somewhere behind her, and turned quickly to find a smiling negro woman close behind her.

"I likes Massa Philip myse'f," declared the woman, "an' I wishes I could see him jus' a minute," and her smile disappeared. "I'se shuah Massa Philip won' let 'em sell Dinkie, or lash her either," and putting her apron over her face the woman began to cry.

"He won't! I heard him say he wouldn't have it," Sylvia assured her eagerly. "Don't cry, Dinkie," and she patted the woman's arm.

Dinkie let her apron fall and looked eagerly at Sylvia.

"You'se the little Yankee missy, ain't you?" she questioned. "I hear say that Yankees don't believe in selling black folks."

"They don't; I'm sure they don't. I'll run right back and tell Philip you want to see him," replied Sylvia. "You stay right here by this tree," she added, pointing to a big live-oak.

"Yas, Missy, I thanks you," replied the woman.

Sylvia ran back toward the house as fast as she could go. She could see the ponies standing before the house, a small negro boy holding their bridle-reins. The girls were on the steps waiting for her.

"I mustn't let them know that Dinkie wants to see Philip," she thought, as the girls called out that they had been looking everywhere for her. At that moment the two boys came along the piazza.

"Philip is going to teach you how to mount, and how to hold your reins, Sylvia," said Flora.

Grace and Sylvia were to ride the white ponies, and Flora was to ride a small brown horse which her mother usually rode.

Philip came slowly down the steps. He looked very sober, and Sylvia was sure that he was thinking about Dinkie. "I don't believe he thinks slavery is right," she thought, as Philip raised his cap, and asked if she was ready to mount "Snap," the pony which she was to ride.

Flora and Grace were already mounted, and trotted slowly off. Sylvia and Philip were alone on the driveway.

"Dinkie wants to see you. She's waiting down by the oak, beyond the lake," said Sylvia. "And don't let her be whipped," she added.

The boy looked up at her quickly.

"Don't tell the girls that she sent for me," he replied. "Dinkie shan't be whipped, or sold either." He did not thank Sylvia for her message, and she was glad that he did not. With a brief word of direction as to the proper manner of holding the reins, he turned toward the lake, and Sylvia's pony trotted slowly down the drive to where Flora and Grace were waiting.

Flora led the way past the stables, and down a broad path which led to the negro quarters. The ponies went at a slow pace, as Flora wanted to be sure that Sylvia was not afraid, and that she was enjoying her first ride.

"The corn-shucking will be here," she said, pointing with her pretty gold-mounted whip to a number of corn-cribs. "They will bring the corn in from the fields, and we will come down in good season."

"And the moon will be full to-night," said Grace, beginning to sing:

> "'De jay-bird hunt de sparrer-nes',
>   All by de light of de moon.
> De bee-martin sail all 'roun',
>   All by de light of de moon.
> De squirrel he holler from de top of de tree;
> Mr. Mole he stay in de groun',
> Oh, yes! Mr. Mole he stay in de groun'——-'"

Sylvia listened and smiled as she looked at the happy faces of her friends. But she could not forget Dinkie, and wondered if Philip could really protect the unhappy woman from a whipping, and prevent her being sold away from her children.

As they passed the cabins of the negroes the children ran out bobbing and smiling to their young mistress, and Flora called out a friendly greeting.

"Father's going to sell a lot of those niggers," she said carelessly. "They eat more than they're worth."

"But won't their mothers feel dreadfully to let them go?" ventured Sylvia.

"Of course they will," declared Grace, before Flora could respond. "And I do think it's a shame. Did you know Uncle Robert is going to sell Estralla?" she asked turning to Sylvia.

Sylvia's grasp on the reins loosened, and she nearly lost her seat on the broad back of the fat pony.

"What for?" she questioned, thinking to herself that Estralla should not be sold away from her home and mother if she, Sylvia, could prevent it.

"Oh, Uncle's agent says she isn't of any use, and he can get a good price for her. He would have sold her last month if your mother had not taken her in. I expect Aunt Connie will be half crazy, for all her other children are gone," said Grace.

"We mustn't ride too far this time," Flora interrupted, "because it's Sylvia's first ride. Hasn't she done well? Do you suppose you can turn the pony?"

"Yes, indeed," answered Sylvia, drawing the left rein so tightly that the little pony swung round before Flora had time to give a word of direction. As they were now headed toward home "Snap" went off at a good pace well in advance of the others. It was all Sylvia could do to keep her seat, but she was not frightened, and when the pony raced up the driveway and came to a standstill directly in front of the piazza steps she was laughing with delight. For the moment she had quite forgotten Dinkie and Estralla.

CHAPTER VII

SYLVIA SEES A GHOST

"It was splendid," declared Sylvia as Grace and Flora dismounted and the three little friends entered the house. Flora's black "Mammy" was waiting for them on the piazza.

"Thar's some 'freshments fur yo' in de dinin'-room," she said; and the girls were glad for the cool milk and the tiny frosted cakes which a negro girl served them. Sylvia wondered if Flora ever did anything for herself; for there seemed to be so many negro servants who were on the alert to wait upon all the white people at the "big house."

"Come up to my room, and rest until it's time to dress for supper," said Flora.

Flora's room was just across the hall from the one where Grace and Sylvia were to sleep. Instead of a small white bed like theirs there was a big bed of dark mahogany with four tall, high posts. The bed was so high that there was a cushioned step beside it. The portrait of a lady hung over a beautiful inlaid desk, and Flora pointed to it with evident pride.

"That's my great-grandmother; and her father built

this house. My mother says that she was Lady Caroline, and that she was so beautiful that whenever she went to Charleston people would run after her coach just to look at her," and Flora looked at her companions expectantly, quite forgetting that she had told them the story before.

"Oh, Flora! Every time I come out here you tell me about your wonderful great-grandmother," said Grace, "and you used to tell me that her ghost haunted this house."

"Well, it does," declared Flora.

Sylvia had never heard of Lady Caroline's ghost. "Do tell me about it, Flora," she urged.

There was a wide cushioned seat with many pillows beneath the windows, and here the girls established themselves very comfortably.

"Yes, tell Sylvia the story," said Grace, piling up several cushions behind her back. "Of course it isn't true, but it's thrilling."

"It is true," persisted Flora. "My mother says that her own governess saw Lady Caroline's ghost. And that she had on the very hat she has on in the portrait, and the same blue dress and lace collar. You know there's a secret stairway in this house. It leads from one of the closets in your room down to a closet in my father's library and out-of-doors, and Lady Caroline's ghost always comes in that way."

Sylvia looked up at the beautiful pictured face with a little shiver. "I guess that the governess dreamed it," she said.

"Of course she did," declared Grace. "I think you look like that picture, Flora," she added.

"Well, whether you believe it or not, everybody knows that this is a haunted house," persisted Flora. "Why, there is an account of it in a book."

But Grace shook her head laughingly. "Flora, show Sylvia your lovely lace-work," she said.

Flora nodded, but Sylvia was sure that she was not pleased at Grace's refusal to believe in the ghost.

"Mammy! Mam-m-e-e," called Flora, and in a moment the black woman stood bobbing and smiling in the doorway.

"Bring my lace-work," said Flora.

"Yas, Missy," and Mammy trotted across the room to a little table in the further corner and brought Flora a covered basket. She opened it and set it down in front of her little mistress.

"Do's yo' want anyt'ing else, Missy Flora?" she asked.

"If I do I'll call," replied the little girl, and Mammy again disappeared.

The basket was lined with rose-colored silk, and there were little pockets all around it. In the centre lay a cushion on which was a lace pattern defined by delicate threads and tiny circles of pins. A little strip of finished lace was rolled up in a bit of tissue paper. Flora took off the paper. "See, it is the jessamine pattern," she explained. "My mother's governess was a Belgian lady, and she taught my mother how to make lace and my mother taught me."

"I wish I could make lace," said Sylvia. "It would be lovely to make some for a present for my mother."

"Of course it would. I'll teach you this winter," promised the good-natured Flora; "let me see your hands. You know a lace-maker's hands must be as smooth as silk, because any roughness would catch the delicate threads."

Sylvia's hands were still scratched and roughed from her fall in Miss Rosalie's garden and her scramble over the wall, and Flora shook her head. "You'll have to wait awhile. And you must wear gloves every time you go out, and wash your hands in milk every night," she said very seriously. "Now I'll show you my embroidery. Mam-m-e-e! Mam-m-e-e," and another basket was brought and opened. This basket was also lined with rose-colored silk, but the silk had delicate green vines running over it. On the inside of the cover, held in place by tiny straps, were two pairs of shining scissors with gold handles, a gold-mounted emery bag, shaped like a strawberry, an embroidery stiletto of ivory, and a gold thimble.

Flora lifted out the embroidery frame, and putting on her thimble took a few exact, dainty stitches in the collar.

"What lovely work you can do, Flora!" exclaimed Sylvia. "Don't you ever play dolls?" remembering her own cherished dolls in their small chairs in the corner of her room at home.

"Oh, I used to," replied Flora, "but since I began school at Miss Patten's I don't seem to care about dolls."

"Flora can play on the harp," announced Grace.

"Oh, only just a little," responded Flora quickly.

"I think Flora can do more things than any girl I ever knew," declared Sylvia admiringly; "and I was just thinking that the servants did everything in the world."

Flora laughed. "You never lived on a plantation, or you couldn't think that. Why, my mother works more than Mammy ever did. She has to tell all the house darkies what to do, and see that all the hands have clothes, and that the fruits are preserved. Why, she's always busy," replied Flora. "And of course ladies have to know how to do things," she concluded.

When Grace and Sylvia went to their own room Flora went with them. "I'll show you where that secret staircase is," she said, and opening the closet door pressed on a broad panel which moved slowly.

"There," and Flora drew Sylvia near so she could look down a dark narrow stairway.

"But that isn't seeing a ghost," Grace said laughingly.

Flora made no answer, and Sylvia wondered why her little hostess looked so serious.

Supper was ready when the girls came downstairs, and as soon as it was over the family all started off toward the field where the corn-shucking was to be. Philip walked with Flora and Sylvia, a little behind the others, and Sylvia hoped she would have a chance to ask him about Dinkie.

The house servants were carrying down big baskets filled with food; for as soon as the corn was shucked there would be a supper for the workers.

The corn was brought close to the corn-cribs and heaped up in great piles. The negroes were already busily at work, and before Sylvia and her friends reached the field they could hear laughter, the sound of a banjo, and singing; and as they came into the open space Sylvia gave a little exclamation of surprise. A dozen or more negroes were dancing up and down in front of the workers, singing:

> "I know dat supper will be big,
>   Shuck dat corn before you eat.
> I think I smell a fine roast pig,
>   Shuck dat corn before you eat.
>
> I smell de supper, dat I do,
>   Shuck dat corn before you eat.
> On de table will be fine stew,
>   Shuck dat corn before you eat."

When they finished singing they sat down and began work, and other negroes jumped up and sang other songs.

"They all look as happy as can be," exclaimed Sylvia.

"Well, tell them they're going to be sold and they won't be very happy," grumbled Philip, who stood beside her. "I can't get my mother to promise not to sell Dinkie," he continued, as Flora turned to speak to Grace, "but she has promised not to let her be whipped."

Sylvia's delight in the negroes and their songs all vanished.

"But you said you wouldn't let her be sold. I told her you said so," she responded.

"You may be sure Dinkie won't be sold," the boy declared. "I know when Father comes home he will give me Dinkie if I ask him, and I mean to ask him first thing. My! I hate this buying and selling darkies. I almost wish I lived in Boston," he concluded.

It was rather late when Mrs. Hayes led the way back to the house, and Grace declared that she was almost too sleepy to walk up-stairs. But Sylvia was not at all sleepy. After the colored girl had helped them prepare for bed, blown out the candle, and left the room, she lay watching the shadows of the moving vines on the wall. She wished she was at home, for who knew but that Estralla's master might sell her before she returned. Sylvia wondered what she could do to protect the little girl. "I might hide her," she thought; but what place would be secure? Suddenly she remembered something that she had heard Captain Carleton say when she was eating luncheon on that unlucky trip to Fort Sumter. "This fort could make South Carolina give up slavery," he had said. Why, then, of course Estralla would be perfectly safe if she was only at Fort Sumter, concluded the little girl, with a long sigh of relief. "I must get her there just as soon as I get home," she decided.

Then suddenly Sylvia sat straight up in bed. The closet door had swung softly open, and a figure with a big hat and trailing dress stepped out. Sylvia was not frightened. "It's the ghost," she whispered; and leaning across poked Grace, exclaiming: "Grace! Look quick! here is Lady Caroline!"

In an instant Grace was wide awake.

"Where?" she demanded, in a frightened voice, clutching Sylvia's hand.

"Right there! By the closet door," said Sylvia. "Oh! she's gone!"

For as she looked toward the closet the figure had disappeared.

"There, you waked me up for nothing. You dreamed it," declared Grace.

"Oh, I didn't! Truly, I didn't. I haven't been asleep," Sylvia insisted. "It is just as Flora said.

There is a ghost." Just then both the girls heard a startled cry, and a sound as if something had fallen in the room under them.

"What's that?" whispered Grace. "Oh, Sylvia, do you suppose there really is a ghost?"

"Yes, I saw it," declared Sylvia, with such evident satisfaction in her tone that Grace forgot to be frightened. "Well, I guess it fell downstairs,", she chuckled; but in spite of their lack of fear both the little girls were excited over the unusual noise, and Sylvia was sure now that Flora had been right in saying the house was haunted. She wished it was already morning that she might tell Flora all that had happened.

CHAPTER VIII

A TWILIGHT TEA-PARTY

It was late when Grace and Sylvia awoke the following morning, but they were down-stairs before the boys appeared. Mrs. Hayes greeted them smilingly, but she said that Flora was not well and that Mammy would take her breakfast to her up-stairs.

"After breakfast you must go up and stay with her a little while," said Mrs. Hayes.

"Why, Flora was never ill in her life," declared Ralph; "what's the matter?"

She is not really ill, but she fell over something last night and bruised her arm and shoulder, so that she feels lame and tired, and I thought a few hours in bed would be the best thing for her," explained Mrs. Hayes. "Mammy doesn't seem to know just how it happened," she concluded.

Sylvia and Grace had talked over the "ghost" before coming down-stairs. Grace had tried her best to convince Sylvia that she had really dreamed "Lady Caroline," but Sylvia insisted that a figure in a wide plumed hat and a trailing gown had really stepped out of the closet.

"The moon was shining right where she stood. I saw her just as plainly as I could see you when you sat up in bed," Sylvia declared. But both the girls agreed that it would be best not to say anything about "Lady Caroline" until they had told Flora.

After breakfast Mammy came to tell the visitors that Flora was ready to see them.

"But jus' for a little while," she added, as she opened the door of Flora's chamber.

Flora was bolstered up in bed, and had on a dainty dressing-gown of pink muslin tied with white ribbons. But there was a bandage about her right wrist, and a soft strip of cotton was bound about her head.

"Oh, girls! It's too bad that I can't help you to have a good time to-day," she said, "and all because I was so clumsy."

Both the girls assured her that it was a good time just to be at the Hayes plantation.

"Flora! There is a ghost! Just as you said! I saw it. Just about midnight," said Sylvia.

"Truly!" exclaimed Flora, in rather a faint voice.

"Yes. And it was Lady Caroline. For it wore a big hat, like the one in the picture, and its dress trailed all about it," replied Sylvia.

"Then I guess Grace will believe this *is* a haunted house," said Flora, a little triumphantly.

"I didn't see it," said Grace. "And, truly, I believe Sylvia just dreamed it."

Flora sat up in bed suddenly.

"Sylvia did not dream it. I know she saw it," she declared.

"Well, perhaps so. But I didn't," and Grace laughed good-naturedly; but Flora turned her face from them and began to cry.

"After my being hurt, and——" she sobbed, but stopped quickly.

Sylvia and Grace looked at each other in amazement.

"It's because she is ill. And she's disappointed because you didn't see Lady Caroline," Sylvia whispered. In a moment Flora looked up with a little smile.

"I am so silly," she said. "You must forgive me. But I'm sure Sylvia did see ——"

"I begin to think she did," Grace owned laughingly. She had happened to look toward the open closet and had seen certain things which made her quite ready to own that Flora might be right. But she was rather serious and silent for the rest of the visit. Before they left Flora's room Flora asked Sylvia not to tell anyone that she had seen a "ghost." "You see, the boys would laugh, and no one but me really believes the house is haunted," she explained.

Of course Sylvia promised, but she was puzzled by Flora's request.

It was decided that Ralph and Philip should ride back to Charleston that afternoon when Uncle Chris drove the little visitors home, and that Flora should stay at the plantation with her mother for a day or two.

Sylvia had enjoyed her visit. She had even enjoyed seeing the "ghost," but she was sorry that she could not tell her mother and father of the great adventure. Nevertheless she was glad when the carriage stopped in front of her own home, and she saw Estralla, smiling and happy in the pink gingham dress, waiting to welcome her.

"Sylvia, I'm coming over to-night. I've got something to tell you," Grace said, as the two friends stood for a moment at Sylvia's gate, after they had thanked Uncle Chris, and said good-bye to Sylvia's brothers.

Grace was so serious that Sylvia wondered what it could be. "It isn't that Estralla is going to be sold right away, is it?" she asked anxiously.

"No. I'll tell you after supper," Grace responded and ran on to her own home.

Sylvia's mother and father were interested to hear all that she had to tell them about the corn-shucking, and of the wonderful cake with its palmetto flag. She told them about poor Dinkie, and what Philip had said: that Dinkie should not be sold away from her children, or whipped.

Mr. Fulton seemed greatly pleased with Sylvia's account of her visit. He said Philip was a fine boy, and that there were many like him in South Carolina.

They had just finished supper when Grace appeared, and the two little girls went up to Sylvia's room.

"What is it, Grace?" Sylvia asked eagerly. "I can't think what you want to tell me that makes you look so sober."

Grace looked all about the room and then closed the door, not seeing a little figure crouching in a shadowy corner.

"I wouldn't want anybody else to hear. It's about the ghost," she whispered. "I know all about it. It was Flora herself! Yes, it was!" she continued quickly. "When we were in her room this morning I saw a big hat with a long feather on it, hanging on her closet door, and a long blue skirt, one of her mother's. They weren't there yesterday, for the door was open, just as it was to-day."

"Well, what of that?" asked Sylvia.

"Oh, Sylvia! Can't you see?" Grace asked impatiently. "Flora dressed up in her mother's things, and then came up the stairs to our room. She was determined to make us think she had a truly ghost in her house. Then when you called out, she got frightened and stumbled on the stairs. You know we heard someone fall and cry out. Of course it was Flora. Nobody seems to know how she got hurt. The minute I saw that plumed hat I knew just the trick she had played. I knew there wasn't a ghost," Grace concluded triumphantly.

Sylvia felt almost disappointed that it had not really been "Lady Caroline." She wondered why Flora had wanted to deceive them.

"I don't think it was fair," she said slowly.

"Of course it wasn't fair. I wouldn't have believed that a Charleston girl would do such a mean trick," declared Grace. "Of course, as we were her company, we can't let her know that we have found her out."

"Perhaps she meant to tell us, anyway," suggested Sylvia hopefully. "I'm sure she did. She thought it would make us laugh."

"Well, then why didn't she?" asked Grace.

Sylvia's face clouded; she could not answer this question, but she was sure that Flora had not meant to frighten or really deceive them, and she wanted to defend her absent friend.

"Well, Grace, we know Flora wouldn't do anything mean. And, you see, she got hurt, and so she's just waiting to get well before she tells us of the joke. You wait and see. Flora will tell us just as soon as we see her again."

There was a little note of entreaty in Sylvia's voice, as if she were pleading with Grace not to blame Flora.

"I know one thing, Sylvia. You wouldn't do anything mean, if you are a Yankee," Grace declared warmly. "What's that noise?" she added quickly.

The room was shadowy in the gathering twilight, and the two little girls had been sitting near the window. As Grace spoke they both turned quickly, for there was a sudden noise of an overturned chair in the further corner of the room, and they could see a dark figure sprawling on the floor.

Before Sylvia could speak she heard the little wailing cry which Estralla always gave when in trouble, and then: "Don't be skeered, Missy! It's nobuddy. I jes' fell over your doll-ladies."

"Oh, Estralla! You haven't broken my dolls! What were you up here for, anyway?" and Sylvia quite forgot all her plans to rescue Estralla as she ran toward her.

The "doll-ladies," as the little darky girl had always called Sylvia's two china dolls which sat in two small chairs in front of a doll's table in one corner of the room, were both sprawling on the floor, their chairs upset, and the little table with its tiny tea-set overturned. Grace lit the candles on Sylvia's bureau, while Sylvia picked up her treasured dolls, "Molly" and "Polly," which her Grandmother Fulton had sent her on her last birthday.

"I wuz up here, jest a-sittin' an' a-lookin' at 'em, Missy," wailed Estralla. "I never layed hand on 'em. An' when you an' Missy Grace comes in I da'sent move. An' then when I does move I tumbles over. I 'spec' now I'll get whipped."

"Keep still, Estralla. You know you won't get whipped," replied Sylvia, finding that Molly and Polly had not been hurt by their fall, and that none of the little dishes were broken.

"You ought to tell her mother to whip her. She's no business up here," said Grace.

"Don't, Grace!" Sylvia exclaimed. "We don't get whipped every time we make a mistake. And Estralla hasn't anything of her own. Just think, your Uncle Robert can sell her away from her own mother. You said yourself that you didn't think that was fair."

Estralla had scrambled to her feet and now stood looking at the little white girls with a half-frightened look in her big eyes.

"Oh, Missy! I ain't gwine to be sold, be I?" she whispered.

Sylvia put her arm around Estralla's shoulders. "No!" she said, "you shall not be sold. Now, don't look so frightened. We will have a tea-party for Molly and Polly, and you shall wait on them. Run down and ask your mother to give us some little cakes."

Estralla was off in an instant, and while she was away Sylvia and Grace spread the little table, brought cushions from the window-seats and advised Molly and Polly to forgive the disturbance.

When Mrs. Fulton came up-stairs a little later to tell Grace that her black Mammy had come to take her home she found three very happy little girls. Sylvia and Grace were being entertained at tea by Misses Molly and Polly, while Estralla with shining eyes and a wide smile carried tiny cups and little cakes to the guests, and chuckled delightedly over the clever things which Sylvia and Grace declared Molly and Polly had said.

"A candle-light tea-party," exclaimed Mrs. Fulton, as she came into the room and smiled down on the happy group.

"Perhaps Flora will own up," Grace said, as the two girls followed Mrs. Fulton down the stairs. "Anyway, you are mighty fair about it, and you're good to that stupid little darky."

Oh, Estralla isn't stupid. Not a bit," replied Sylvia laughingly.

Estralla, who was carefully putting the little table in order, heard Sylvia's defense of her, and for a moment she stood very straight, holding one of the tiny cups in each hand.

"I jes' loves Missy Sylvia, I do. I jes' wish ez how I could do somethin' so she'd know how I loves her," and two big tears rolled down the black cheeks of the little slave girl who had known so little of kindness or of joy.

CHAPTER IX

TROUBLESOME WORDS

IT was a week after Sylvia's visit to the Hayes plantation before Flora returned to school. A heavy rain had made the roads nearly impassable, and a little scar on Flora's forehead reminded Sylvia and Grace of her unlucky tumble. On Flora's first appearance at school Sylvia was confident that she would at once confess her part in "Lady Caroline's" appearance, and at recess she and Grace were eager to walk with Flora. It was now the first of November, but the air was warm and the garden had many blossoming plants and shrubs.

Flora said that she was glad to be back at school. She told the girls that her father had returned from a northern trip and that he had given Dinkie and her children to Philip.

"Phil teased him so that Father was tired of hearing him. He said Phil was a regular abolitionist," Flora explained with her pretty smile.

"What's an abbylitionzist?" asked Grace.

"Ask Sylvia. I heard my father say that Sylvia's father was one," answered Flora.

"I don't know. But my father is a Congregationalist," replied Sylvia. "Perhaps that's what your father meant."

"No, it's something about not believing in having slaves, I know that much," said Flora.

"Who would do our work then?" questioned Grace.

Flora could not answer this question. Sylvia resolved to ask Miss Rosalie at question time the meaning of this new word. If her father and Philip Hayes were "abolitionists," she was quite sure the word meant something very brave and fine.

"What about Miss Flora and her ghost now?" Grace found a chance to whisper, as they entered the school-room. "She doesn't mean to own up."

"Wait, she will," was Sylvia's response as she took her seat.

When question time came Sylvia was ready. She stood up smiling and eager, and Miss Rosalie smiled back. She had grown fond of her little pupil from Boston, and thought to herself that Sylvia was really becoming almost like a little southern girl in her graceful ways and pleasant smile.

"What is your question, Sylvia?" she asked.

"If you please, Miss Rosalie, what does 'abolitionist' mean?"

Some of the older girls exchanged startled looks, and May Bailey barely restrained a laugh. Probably Grace and Sylvia were the only girls in school who had not heard the word used as a term of reproach against the people of the northern states who wished to do away with slavery.

Miss Rosalie's smile faded, but she responded without a moment's hesitation:

"Why, an 'abolitionist' is a person who wishes to destroy some law or custom."

There was a little murmur among the other pupils, but Grace and Sylvia looked at each other with puzzled eyes. Philip did not wish to "destroy" anything, thought Sylvia; he only wanted to protect Dinkie. And she was sure that her father would not destroy anything, unless it was something which would harm people. So it was a puzzled Sylvia who came home from school that day. She decided that her father could answer a question much better than Miss Rosalie, and resolved to ask him the meaning of the word.

"Come up-stairs, Estralla," she said, finding the little negro girl at the gate as usual waiting for her. "I have some things my mother said I could give you."

Estralla followed happily. She didn't care very much what it might be that Missy Sylvia would give her, it was delight enough for Estralla to follow after her. But when the little girl saw the things spread out on Sylvia's bed she exclaimed aloud:

"Does you mean, Missy, dat I'se to pick out somethin'? Well, then I chooses the shoes. I never had no shoes."

"They are all for you," said Sylvia, lifting up a pretty blue cape and holding it toward Estralla.

"My lan'!" whispered Estralla.

There was a dress of blue delaine with tiny white dots, two pretty white aprons, the blue cape, and shoes and stockings, beside some of Sylvia's part-worn underwear. She had begged her mother to let her give the little darky these things, and Mrs. Fulton had been glad that her little daughter wished to do so.

"Estralla has never had *anything*," Sylvia had urged, "and she is always afraid of something. Of being whipped or sold. And I would like to see her have clothes like other girls."

Estralla wanted to try on the shoes at once, and when she found that they fitted very comfortably, she chuckled and laughed with delight. Neither of the girls heard a rap at the door, and both were surprised when Aunt Connie, who had opened the door and stood waiting, exclaimed:

"Fo' lan's sake! W'at you lettin' that darky dress up in you' clo'es fer, Missy Sylvia?"

"They are her own clothes now, Aunt Connie," Sylvia explained. "My mother said I might give them to her."

For a moment the negro woman stood silent. Then she put her hands up to her face and began to cry, very quietly. Estralla's laughter vanished. She wondered if her mammy was going to tell her that she could not keep the things.

" 'Scusie, Missy," muttered Aunt Connie; "you'se an angel to my po' little gal. An' I'se 'bliged to you. But I'se feared the chile won't wear 'em long. Massa Robert Waite's man sez he's gwine sell her off right soon."

"He cyan't do no sech thing. Missy Sylvia won't let him," declared Estralla, who was perfectly sure that "Missy Sylvia" could do whatever she wished. With a pair of shoes on her feet and the blue cape over her shoulders Estralla had more courage. Sylvia's kindness had given the little colored girl a hope of happier days.

"Aunt Connie, I'll do all I can for Estralla," said Sylvia.

"Will you, Missy? Then ask yo' pa not to let Estralla be sold," pleaded Aunt Connie.

Sylvia promised, and Aunt Connie went off smilingly. But Sylvia wondered if her father could prevent Mr. Robert Waite from selling the negro girl.

"Estralla," she said very soberly, "I have promised that you shall not be sold, and I will ask my father. But if he cannot do anything, we will have to do something ourselves. Will you do whatever I tell you?"

"Oh, yas indeed, Missy," Estralla answered eagerly.

"Well, I'll ask Father to-night. And to-morrow morning you bring up my hot water, and I'll tell you what he says. But don't be frightened, anyway," said Sylvia.

"I ain't skeered like I used to be," responded Estralla. "Yo' see, Missy, I feels jes' as if you was my true fr'en'."

"I'll try to be," Sylvia promised.

Estralla went off happy with her new possessions, and Sylvia turned to the window, and looked off across the beautiful harbor toward the forts. She had heard her father say, that very noon, that South Carolina would fight to keep its slaves, and she wondered if the soldiers in Fort Moultrie would not fight to set the black people free. She remembered that her father had said that Fort Sumter was the property of the United States; and, for some reason which she could not explain even to herself, she was sure that Estralla would be safe there. If Mr. Robert Waite really meant to sell her, Sylvia again resolved to find some way to get the little slave girl to Fort Sumter.

When Estralla brought the hot water the next morning she found a very sober little mistress. For Sylvia's father had not only explained the meaning of the word "abolitionist" as being the name the southerners had given to the men who were determined that slavery of other men, whatever their color, should end, but he had told his little daughter that he could do nothing to prevent the sale of the little colored girl, and that not even at Fort Sumter would she be safe. Sylvia had not gone to sleep very early. She lay awake thinking of Estralla. "Suppose somebody could sell me away from my mother," she thought, ready to cry even at such a possibility. Sylvia knew that Aunt Connie had been whipped because she had rebelled against parting with her older children, and there was no Philip to take Aunt Connie's part.

"Mornin', Missy," said Estralla, coming into the room, and setting down the pitcher of hot water very carefully. She had on the pink gingham with one of the white aprons, and as she stood smiling and neat at the foot of Sylvia's bed, she looked very different from the clumsy little darky who had tumbled into the room a few weeks ago. Sylvia smiled back. "Estralla, I want you to be sure to come up-stairs to-night after the house is all quiet. Don't tell your mother, or anybody," she said very soberly.

"All right, Missy," agreed Estralla, sure that what-ever Missy Sylvia asked was right.

Sylvia said nothing more, but dressed and went down to breakfast. She heard her father say that he feared that South Carolina would secede from the United States, and she repeated the word aloud: "'Secede'? What does that mean?" She began to think the world was full of difficult words.

"In this case it means that the State of South Car-olina wishes to give up her rights as one of the States of the Union," Mr. Fulton explained, "but we hope she will give up slavery instead," he concluded.

Grace was at the gate as Sylvia came out ready for school, and called out a gay greeting.

"What are you so sober about, Sylvia?" she asked as they walked on together.

CHAPTER X

THE PALMETTO FLAG

WHEN Sylvia had told Estralla to come to her room that night, she had determined to find a way to get the little negro to a place of safety. Sylvia did not know that a negro was, in those far-off days, the property of his master as much as a horse or a dog, and that wherever the negro might go his master could claim him and punish him for trying to escape. Any person aiding a slave to escape could also be punished by law.

All Sylvia thought of was to have Estralla protected, and she was quite sure that a United States fort could protect one little negro girl. Nevertheless she was troubled and worried as to how she could carry out her plan; but she resolved not to tell Grace.

As usual Flora was waiting at Miss Patten's gate for her friends. She was wearing a pretty turban hat, and pinned in front was a fine blue cockade, to which Flora pointed and said: "Look, girls. This is the Secession Cockade. Ralph gave it to me," she explained; "all loyal Carolinians ought to wear it, Ralph says."

"What does it mean to wear one?" asked Sylvia.

"Oh, it means that you believe South Carolina has a right to keep its slaves, and sell them, of course; and if the United States interferes, why, Carolinians will teach them a lesson," Flora explained grandly, repeating the explanation her father had given her that very morning.

Many of the other girls wore blue cockades, and a palmetto flag was hung behind Miss Rosalie's desk.

"Young ladies," said Miss Rosalie, "I have hung South Carolina's flag where you can all see it. You all know that a flag is an emblem. Our flag means the glory of our past and the hope of the future. I will ask you all to rise and salute this flag!"

The little girls all stood, and each raised her right hand. All but Sylvia. Flushed and unhappy, with downcast eyes, she kept her seat. This was not the "Stars and Stripes," the flag she had been taught to love and honor. She knew that the palmetto flag stood for slavery. Sylvia did not know what Miss Rosalie would say to her, and, even worse than her teacher's disapproval, she was sure that her schoolmates, perhaps even Grace and Flora, would dislike and blame her for not saluting their flag.

But she was soon to realize just how serious was her failure to salute the palmetto flag. Miss Rosalie came down the aisle and laid a note on Sylvia's desk.

It was very brief: "You may go home at recess. Take your books and go quietly without a word to any of the

"RISE AND SALUTE THIS FLAG!"

other pupils. You may tell your parents that I do not care to have you as a pupil for another day."

As Sylvia read these words the tears sprang to her eyes. It was all she could do not to sob aloud. She dared not look at the other girls. She held a book before her face, and only hoped that she could keep back the tears until recess-time.

But not for a moment did Sylvia wish that she had saluted a flag which stood for the protection of slavery. Miss Rosalie had said that a flag was an "emblem," and even in her unhappiness Sylvia knew that the emblem of the United States stood for justice and liberty.

When the hour of recess came Sylvia had her books neatly strapped, and, as Miss Rosalie had directed, she left the room quietly without one word to any of the other girls. She had nearly reached the gate when she heard steps close behind her and Grace's voice calling: "Sylvia, Sylvia, dear," and Grace's arm was about her. "It's a mean shame," declared the warm-hearted little southern girl, "and flag or no flag, I'm your true friend."

"Grace! Grace!" called Miss Rosalie, and before Sylvia could respond her loyal playmate had turned obediently back to the house.

Sylvia stepped out on the street, her eyes a little blurred by tears, but greatly comforted by Grace's assuring words of friendship.

She did not want to go home and tell her mother what had happened, and show her Miss Patten's note, for she knew that her mother would be troubled and unhappy.

Suddenly she decided to go to her father's warehouse and tell him, and go home with him at noon. She was sure her father would think she had done right.

She turned and walked quickly down King Street, and in a short time she was near the wharves and could see the long building where her father stored the cotton he purchased from the planters. The wharves were piled high with boxes and bales, and there were small boats coming in to the wharves, and others making ready to depart.

Sylvia could see her father's boat close to the wharf near the warehouse. "I wish I could take that boat and carry Estralla off to Fort Sumter," she thought.

A good-natured negro led her to Mr. Fulton's office, and before her father could say a word Sylvia was in the midst of her story. She told of the blue cockades that the other girls wore, of the palmetto flag, and of her failure to salute it, and handed him Miss Patten's note.

Mr. Fulton looked serious and troubled as he listened to his little girl's story. Then he lifted her to his knee, took off her pretty hat, and said:

"Too bad, dear child! But you did right. A little Yankee girl must be loyal to the Stars and Stripes. I am glad you came and told me."

For a moment it seemed to Sylvia that her father had forgotten all about her. He was looking straight out of the window.

While he had not forgotten his little girl he was thinking that Charleston people must be quite ready to take the serious step of urging their State to declare her secession from the United States, and her right to buy and sell human beings as slaves.

He wished that the United States officers at Fort Moultrie could realize that at any time Charleston men might seize Fort Sumter, where there were but few soldiers, and he said aloud: "I ought to warn them."

Sylvia wondered for a moment what her father could mean, but he said quickly: "Jump down and put on your hat. I'm going to sail down to Fort Moultrie and have a talk with my good friends there, and you can come with me."

At this good news Sylvia forgot all her troubles. A sail across the harbor with her father was the most delightful thing that she could imagine. And she held fast to his hand, smiling happily, as they walked down the wharf where the boat was fastened.

Mr. Fulton was beginning to find his position as a northern man in Charleston rather uncomfortable. Many of his southern friends firmly believed that the northern men had no right to tell them that slavery was wrong and must cease. He wished to protect his business interests, or he would have returned to Boston; for it was difficult for him not to declare his own patriotic feeling that Abraham Lincoln, who had just been elected President of the United States, would never permit slavery to continue.

Mr. Fulton sent a darky with a message to Sylvia's mother that he was taking the little girl for a sail to the forts, and in a short time they were on board the *Butterfly*, as Sylvia had named the white sloop, and were going swiftly down the harbor.

"May I steer?" asked Sylvia, and Mr. Fulton smilingly agreed. He was very proud of his little daughter's ability to sail a boat, and although be watched her shape the boat's course, and was ready to give her any needed assistance, he was sure that he could trust her.

As they sailed past Fort Sumter Sylvia could see men at work repairing the fortifications. Over both forts waved the Stars and Stripes.

She made a skilful landing at Fort Moultrie, greatly to the admiration of the sentry on guard. Mr. Fulton and Sylvia went directly to the officers' quarters, which were in the rear of the fort, and where Mrs. Carleton gave Sylvia a warm welcome. She asked the little girl about her school and Sylvia told her what had happened that morning.

"I am not surprised," said Captain Carleton. "I expect any day that Charleston men will take Fort Sumter, and fly the palmetto flag, instead of the Stars and Stripes. If Major Anderson had his way we would

have a stronger force in Fort Sumter, and that is greatly needed."

Major Anderson was the officer in command at Fort
Moultrie. He was a southern man, but a true and loyal
officer of the United States.

When Captain Carleton and Mr. Fulton went out
Mrs. Carleton asked Sylvia if she was sorry to leave the
school, and if she liked her schoolmates. Sylvia was
eager to tell her of all the good times she had enjoyed
with Grace and Flora, and declared that they were her
true friends. Then she told Mrs. Carleton about Estralla, and of her resolve that the little darky girl should
not be separated from Aunt Connie.

"Your best plan, then, will be to go and see Mr.
Robert Waite and ask him. He is a kind-hearted man,
and perhaps he will promise you to let the child stay
with her mother. I hope it will not be long now before
all the slaves will be set free," said Mrs. Carleton.

Before Sylvia could respond Captain Carleton came
hurrying into the room. He had a letter in his hand, and
asked Sylvia to excuse Mrs. Carleton for a moment, and
they left the room together. In a few moments Mrs.
Carleton returned alone, and Sylvia heard Captain Carleton say: "It is worth trying."

"My dear Sylvia, I want you to do something for me;
it is not really for me," she added quickly, "it is for the
United States. Something to help keep the flag flying
over these forts."

"Oh, can I do something like that?" Sylvia asked eagerly.

"Yes, my dear. Now, listen carefully. Here is a letter which Major Anderson wants delivered to a gentleman who will start for Washington to-morrow. If anyone from this fort should be seen visiting that gentleman he would not be allowed to leave Charleston as he plans. If your father, even, should call upon him it would create suspicion. So I am going to ask you to carry this letter to the address written on the envelope, and you must give it into his own hands to-night. Not even your own father will know that you have this letter; so if he should be questioned or watched he will be able to deny knowing of its existence. Are you willing to undertake it?"

"Yes! Yes!" promised Sylvia. "I will carry it safely. The gentleman shall have the letter to-night," and she reached out her hand to take it.

But Mrs. Carleton shook her head. "No, my dear, I will pin it safely inside your dress. It would not do for you to be seen leaving the fort with a letter in your hand."

CHAPTER XI

SYLVIA CARRIES A MESSAGE

MRS. FULTON did not seem surprised to hear of Sylvia's dismissal from Miss Patten's school because of her failure to salute the palmetto flag. She did not say very much of the occurrence that afternoon, when Sylvia returned from the fort, for she wanted Sylvia to think as pleasantly as possible of her pretty teacher. But she was surprised that Sylvia herself did not have more to say about the affair.

But Sylvia's own thoughts were so filled by the mysterious letter which was pinned inside her dress, with wondering how she could safely deliver it without the knowledge of anyone, that she hardly thought of school. For the time she had even forgotten Estralla.

"What do you say to becoming a teacher yourself, Sylvia dear?" her mother asked, as they sat together in the big sunny room which overlooked the harbor.

"When I grow up?" asked Sylvia.

Mrs. Fulton smiled. Sylvia "grown up" seemed a long way in the future.

"No—that is too far away," she answered. "I was thinking that perhaps you would like to teach

Estralla to read and write. You could begin to-morrow, if you wished."

"Yes, indeed! Mother, you think of everything," declared Sylvia. "Why, that will be better than going to school!"

"But we must not let your own studies be neglected," her mother reminded her, "so after you have given Estralla a morning lesson each day you and I will study together and keep up with Grace and Flora. By the way, Flora was here just before you and your father reached home; she was very sorry not to see you, and I have asked Flora and Grace to come to supper to-morrow night."

Sylvia began to think that a world without school was going to be a very pleasant world after all. She was sure that it would be great fun to teach Estralla, and to have lessons with her mother was even better than reciting to pretty Miss Rosalie; and, beside this, her best friends were coming to supper the next night, so she had many pleasant things to think of, which was exactly what her mother had planned. Her father had said that she might ask Grace to go sailing with them in the *Butterfly* in a day or two; and now Sylvia resolved to ask if she might not ask Flora as well, and perhaps Estralla could go, too. So it was no wonder that she ran up-stairs singing:

> "There 's a good time coming,
>   It's almost here,"—

greatly to the satisfaction of her father and mother, who had feared that she would be very unhappy over the school affair. They were sorry it had happened, but they could not blame Sylvia.

"Oh, Missy Sylvia, here I is," and as Sylvia set her candle on the table, Estralla stood smiling before her.

"Oh!" exclaimed Sylvia with such surprise that the little darky looked at her wonderingly.

"Yo' tells me to come, an' here I is," she repeated. "You tells me," and Estralla sniffed as if ready to give her usual wails, "that you'se gwine to stop my bein' sold off from my mammy. How you gwine to stop it, Missy?"

For a moment Sylvia was tempted to tell Estralla that it couldn't be helped, as long as South Carolina believed in slavery. But Estralla's sad eyes and pleading look made her resolve again to protect this little slave girl against injustice. So she replied quickly:

"That is my secret. But don't you worry. Some day, very soon, I shall tell you all about it. You know, Estralla, that you need not be afraid. And what do you think! I am not going to school any more."

Estralla's face had brightened. She was always quite ready to smile, but she could not understand why Sylvia had wanted her to come so mysteriously to her room.

"And I am going to teach you to read and write," Sylvia added.

"Is you, Missy?" Estralla responded in a half-frightened whisper. Now, she thought, she knew all about Missy Sylvia's reasons for the secret visit. For very few slave-owners allowed anyone to teach the slaves to read and write. Estralla knew this, and it seemed a wonderful thing that Missy Sylvia proposed.

"I'll tell you all about it to-morrow morning," said Sylvia; "now run away," and with a chuckle of delight Estralla closed the door softly behind her. She had been quite ready to run away with Missy Sylvia when she had crept up the stairs earlier in the evening. But to stay safely with her mammy and learn to read seemed a much happier plan to the little darky. If she could read and write! Why, it would be almost as wonderful as it would to be a little white girl, she thought.

Now Sylvia realized, as she stood alone in her safe, pleasant chamber, that as soon as possible she must deliver the letter entrusted to her. If it was to go to Washington it must be some message that was of importance to the officers at Fort Moultrie and Fort Sumter, she thought. Perhaps it might even be something that would help Carolinians to give up slavery; and then Estralla and Aunt Connie, and all the black people she knew and liked, could be safe and have homes of their own.

Sylvia went to the window and peered out. The street and garden lay dark and shadowy. Now and then a dark figure went along the street. The house seemed very quiet. She tiptoed to the closet and took out a brown cape. It was one which she wore on stormy days, and nearly covered her. Then from one of the bureau draw-ers she drew out a long blue silk scarf, and twisted it about her head.

"I can pull the end over my face, and they'll think I'm a darky," she thought, resolved if anyone spoke to her not to answer.

She whispered over the name and address on the letter. She knew that the street led from King Street, and she was sure that she could find it. But it was some distance from home; it would be late before she could get back.

She blew out her candle, opened her chamber door and stood listening. She could not hear a sound, and tiptoed cautiously along the hall to the stairs. What if the door of her mother's room should open, she thought, terrified at such a possibility. What could she say? She had promised not to tell of the letter, and what reason could she give for creeping out of the house at that hour?

But she reached the lower floor safely, and now came the danger of making a noise when opening the door. Sylvia grasped the big key and turned it slowly. Then she pulled at the heavy door, and it swung back easily. She gave a long breath of relief as she stepped out on the piazza. She left the door ajar, so that she could slip in easily on her return. Keeping in the shadow of the trees she reached the street, and now she felt sure that nothing could prevent her from delivering the letter.

She ran swiftly along, now and then meeting someone who glanced wonderingly at the flying little figure. She had reached King Street and was nearly at the street where she was to turn, when suddenly a heavy hand grasped her arm and nearly swung her from her feet.

"Running off, are you? And wearing your mistress's clothes at that, I'll warrant," said a gruff voice. "Wall, now, whose darky are you?"

Sylvia pulled the silken scarf from her face, and even in the glimmer of the dull street-lamp under which the man had drawn her he could see the auburn hair and blue eyes. But he still kept his grasp on her arm. There were slaves who were not black, he knew, and "quality white" girls were not running about Charleston streets alone at night.

"What is your name?" he demanded.

Sylvia looked at him resentfully. "How dare you grab me like this?" she demanded. "Let me go."

The man released his grasp instantly. No darky girl or slave would have spoken like that. He vanished as suddenly as he had appeared, more frightened now than Sylvia herself.

For an instant Sylvia stood quite still. She felt ready to cry, and now walked more slowly. For the first time she realized something of what it must be to be a colored girl.

"If I had been Estralla he could have dragged me off and had me whipped," she thought. "Oh, I must get Mr. Robert Waite to let Estralla stay safe with us."

She was now near her destination, which proved to be a large house right on the street. She knocked at the door several times before it was opened. Then she found herself looking up at a tall man whose white hair and kindly smile gave her confidence.

"Well, little girl, whom do you wish to see?" he asked pleasantly.

"I have a message, I——" began Sylvia, her voice trembling a little. "Are you Mr. Doane?"

"Yes; come in," and he held the door open for her to enter, and then closed and fastened it behind them.

Sylvia drew the letter from its hiding-place and handed it to him, and Mr. Doane slipped it into his pocket.

"Come in, my child, and rest a moment; you are out of breath," he said, leading the way to a small room at the end of the narrow hall.

Sylvia was glad to sit down in a low chair near the table, while Mr. Doane opened the envelope. She could see that there was another letter enclosed, as well as the one which the tall man was reading with such interest.

When he had finished reading the letter he tore it into a great many small pieces. Then he put the enclosed envelope carefully in an inner pocket.

"So you brought me this letter from the fort. Well, you have done what I hope may prove a great service to the Stars and Stripes. I thank you," he said, looking with smiling eyes at the tired little figure in the brown cape.

Then he asked Sylvia her name, and she told him that no one, not even her dear mother, knew that she had brought the message. Before they had finished their talk he had heard all about the blue cockades that the girls had worn at Miss Patten's school, and of Sylvia's refusal to salute the palmetto flag.

"You see I couldn't do that, because it would mean that I believed that Estralla ought to be a slave, and of course I don't believe such a dreadful thing," she explained. So then Mr. Doane heard all about Estralla and Aunt Connie.

Sylvia decided that she liked Mr. Doane even better than Captain Carleton. And when he told her again that by her courage in bringing him the message from the fort, and by her silence in regard to it, that she had done him a great service, as well as a service to those whose only wish for South Carolina was that the State should free herself from slavery, Sylvia forgot all about the long walk through the shadowy streets.

"I wish I had someone to send with you to see you home safely," Mr. Doane said, a little anxiously, as they stood together in the little hallway. "But I am known here, and I fear everything I do is watched. So I must trust that you will be safely cared for."

Before Sylvia could reply, and say that she was not at all afraid to go alone, the outer door rattled as if someone were trying to push it open.

"You have been followed. Run back to the sitting-room," whispered Mr. Doane. "I will open the door."

CHAPTER XII

ESTRALLA HELPS

Sylvia, standing just inside the door of the small room, heard the outer door swing open. She heard Mr. Doane's sharp question, and then a familiar wail.

"Oh! It's Estralla!" she exclaimed, and ran back to the entry.

"It's Estralla! Oh! I'm so glad!" she said.

"Don' you be skeered, Missy Sylvia," said Estralla valiantly. "Dis yere man cyan't take you off'n sell you."

"All Estralla can think of is that somebody is going to be carried off and sold," Sylvia said, turning to Mr. Doane, who stood by looking very serious.

"How did you know where your little mistress was?" he questioned gravely. For if this little darky knew of Sylvia's errand he feared that she might tell others, and so Sylvia would have brought the message from the fort to little purpose. The letter, which was now in Mr. Doane's pocket, was to the Secretary of War in Washington, asking for permission for Major Anderson to take men to Fort Sumter, before the secessionists could occupy it.

"I follers Missy," explained Estralla. "An' when that man grabs her on King Street, I was gwine to chase right home an' get Massa Fulton, but Missy talks brave at him, an' he lets go of her. Oh, Missy! What you doin' of way off here?"

At this question Mr. Doane smiled, realizing that the little negro girl had no knowledge of the message which Sylvia had delivered.

"Well, Estralla, suppose Miss Sylvia came to try and help give you your freedom?" he asked.

"An' my mammy?" demanded Estralla eagerly.

"Why, of course," Mr. Doane replied. "For anything that helps to convince South Carolina that she is wrong will help to free the slaves," he added, turning to Sylvia.

"Now, Estralla, if you love Miss Sylvia, if you want to stay with your mammy, you must never tell of her visit here to-night. Remember!" and Mr. Doane's voice was very stern.

"Estralla won't tell," Sylvia declared confidently; "and I am glad she came to go home with me."

"Shuah I'll do jes' what Missy wants me to," said the little darky.

"Try to let Mrs. Carleton know that I received the letter, and that I hope to reach Washington safely," said Mr. Doane, as he bade Sylvia good-night.

As the door closed behind them Estralla clasped Sylvia's hand.

"W'at dat clock say?" she asked; for one of the city clocks was striking the hour.

"It's twelve o'clock," answered Sylvia.

"Oh! My lan', Missy! Dat's a terrible on-lucky time fer us to be out," whispered Estralla. "Dat's de time w'en witch folks comes a-dancin' an' a-prancin' 'roun' and takes off chilluns."

Sylvia knew that all the negroes believed in witches and all sorts of impossible tales, so Estralla's words did not at all frighten her, but she did wish that she was safe in her own home. The streets were now dark and silent, and black shadows seemed to lurk at every corner as, hand in hand, Estralla and Sylvia ran swiftly along.

"I tells you, Missy, dat it's jes' lucky I comes after you, cos' witch-folks, w'at comes floatin' 'roun' 'bout dis hour of de night, dey ain't gwine to tech us; cos' when dey's two folks holdin' each other hands tight, jes' like we is, dey don't dast to tech us," said Estralla.

"Where were you, Estralla, when I came downstairs?" Sylvia asked.

"I was jes' a-takin' a little sleep on de big rug side of your door, Missy. I'se been a-sleepin' dere dis long time. My mammy lets me. An' when you opens de door I mos' calls out, but didn't. I jes' stan's up quick so's you nebber know I was thar," and Estralla chuckled happily.

Sylvia wondered to herself why Estralla should choose such a hard bed. Then, suddenly, she realized all Estralla's devotion. That the little negro girl had slept there to be near her "fr'en'." She remembered the first time that she had ever seen Estralla, on the morning when she had tumbled in to Sylvia's room and broken the big pitcher, and that even then Estralla had been ready to confess and take the whipping that she was sure would follow, rather than let Sylvia be blamed. She recalled Estralla's effort to rescue her at Fort Sumter on the day Sylvia had run away from Miss Patten's school; and she remembered that it was Estralla who had told Miss Patten the real reason, and so saved her from further trouble.

"Estralla, you have been my true friend," she declared, "and I am going to remember it always. I am going to ask my mother to put a nice little bed for you in your mammy's cabin."

"Don' yo' do that, Missy. I likes sleep in' on de rug," pleaded Estralla.

"Hush, we must creep in without making any noise," responded Sylvia, in a whisper, for they were now directly in front of Sylvia's home.

Noiselessly Estralla led the way.

"Oh, Missy! de door is shut fas'," she whispered, as she endeavored to push it open.

"But it can't be shut," Sylvia answered.

Both the little girls pushed against it, but the door stood fast.

"Oh! What will we do?" half sobbed Sylvia, who was now very tired, and almost too sleepy to think of anything.

"We cyan't get in de back door. My mammy she'd wake up if a rabbit run twixt her cabin an' de kitchen," Estralla whispered back. "I 'spec's I'll hev' to climb up to de winder ober de porch, and comes down and let you in."

"Oh! Can you, Estralla?"

Sylvia's voice was very near to tears. She had forgotten all about the importance of the message she had safely delivered. All she wanted now was to be inside this dear safe house where her mother and father were sleeping, not knowing that their little girl, cold and sleepy, was shut out.

"I 'spec's I can," Estralla answered. "You jes' stay quiet, an' in 'bout four shakes of a lamb's tail I'se gwine to open de door, an' in yo' walks."

There was a little scrambling noise among the stout vines which ran up the pillars of the porch as Estralla started to carry out her plan. A cat, or a fluttering bird, would have hardly made more commotion. Sylvia listened eagerly. Suppose the porch window was fastened? she thought fearfully. It seemed a very long time before the front door opened, and Estralla reached out and clutched at the brown cape.

Noiselessly they crept up the stairs, Estralla leading the way. It was she who opened the door of Sylvia's room, and then with a whispered "Yo'se all right now, Missy," closed it behind her.

Sylvia hung up the brown cape in the closet, and slipped off her dress. She was soon in bed and fast asleep, and it was late the next morning before she awoke—so late that her father had breakfasted and gone to his warehouse; Estralla had been sent on an errand, and Mrs. Fulton decided that Sylvia should have a holiday.

"You seem tired, dear child," she said a little anxiously, as Sylvia said that she did not want to go to walk; that she had rather sit still.

"I guess I am tired," acknowledged the little girl, and was quite content to sit by the window with a story-book, instead of giving Estralla a lesson.

"If it had not been for Estralla I don't know what would have happened to me last night," she thought. She wondered who had closed and fastened the front door, but dared not ask.

Grace and Flora were to come early that afternoon, as soon after school as possible, and Flora had sent Sylvia a note that she would bring her lace-work and give her a lesson. By noon Sylvia felt rested, and was looking eagerly forward to her friends' visit. She began to feel that she was a very fortunate little girl to have had the chance to do something that might help, as Mr. Doane had said, to give the black people their freedom. She only wished that she could tell her mother and father of the midnight journey.

"But I will ask Mrs. Carleton the next time I go to the fort to let me tell Mother," she resolved.

CHAPTER XIII

A HAPPY AFTERNOON

GRACE was the first to arrive, and she declared that she wished that she was in Sylvia's place and need not go to school another day.

The two little friends stood at the window watching for Flora, and it was not long before they saw her coming up the walk, closely followed by her black "Mammy," who was carrying two baskets. One of these seemed very heavy.

"What can be in Mammy's basket, I wonder?" said Grace. "And, look, Sylvia! Flora isn't wearing the blue cockade! That's because she is coming to visit you. She had it on at school this morning."

Flora wore the same pretty velvet turban which she had worn on Sylvia's last day at school. She had on a cape of garnet-colored velvet, and as she came running into the room Sylvia looked at her with admiring eyes.

"You do look so pretty, Flora! And I am so glad to see you. Come up-stairs to my room and take off your things."

"It isn't half the fun going to school now that you don't come, Sylvia," responded Flora, as the three friends went up the broad staircase together. "Mammy," with her baskets, followed them, and when she had helped her little mistress lay aside her cape and hat, Flora said:

"You can go home now, Mammy. And my mother will tell you when to come after me."

"Yas, Missy," responded the old colored woman, and with a curtsey to each of the little girls she left the room.

"What makes your mammy look so sober, Flora?" questioned Grace. "She is usually all smiles; but to-day she hasn't a word to say for herself."

"Oh, the darkies are all stirred up over all this talk about their being set free," Flora answered, "and even Mammy, who was Mother's nurse, and has always been well taken care of, thinks it would be a fine thing for her children and grandchildren to be 'jes' like white folks,'" and Flora laughed scornfully.

"But that needn't make her look sober!" insisted Grace.

"I reckon she's upset because my mother sold two or three little slaves yesterday—Mammy's grandchildren," Flora answered carelessly.

Sylvia could feel her face flushing, and she said over to herself that no matter what Flora said that she, Sylvia, must remember that Flora was her guest. Beside that, had not Flora taken off the blue cockade so that Sylvia would not be reminded of the trouble at school?

But Grace felt no such restraints. She was a southern girl as well as Flora, but she was sorry for the old colored woman.

"Well, I do wish we could keep the pickaninnies until they grow up. It seems a shame when they feel so bad to be sold off to strangers. And some of them are abused too," she said.

"You talk as if they felt just the same as we do, and that's silly," Flora declared; "but Philip talks just the same. He says he is going to give Dinkie her freedom," and she turned toward the two baskets which Mammy had set down with much care near Molly and Polly.

"I brought my lace-work, and Mother has fixed a cushion for you, Sylvia, and one for Grace, too. See! The pattern is begun on each one, and I will give you both lessons until you know as much as I do." As Flora talked she had opened the smaller basket and taken out two square boxes and handed one to each of her friends.

"Open them," she said, nodding smilingly.

The box which she handed to Sylvia was covered with plaited blue silk. It had a narrow edge of gilt braid around the cover. Grace's box was covered with yellow silk, but the boxes were of the same size.

As Sylvia and Grace lifted the covers they smiled and exclaimed happily. The lace cushion lay inside, and in dainty little pockets on each side of the boxes were the delicate threads and materials for the lace. A thimble of gold, with "Sylvia from Flora" engraved around its rim, was in Sylvia's box, and one exactly like it was in Grace's box.

"Oh, Flora Hayes! This is the most beautiful present that ever was!" declared Sylvia; and Grace, holding the box with both hands, was hopping up and down saying over and over: "Flora! You are just like the Golden Princess in a fairy story who gives people what they want most."

"My mother made the boxes herself," Flora explained proudly. "I wanted to give you girls something, and I'm awfully glad you like them." Then Flora stood up quickly.

"Girls! I dressed up in Mother's hat and skirt, that night at the plantation. It wasn't Lady Caroline."

She spoke very rapidly as if she wished to finish as quickly as possible. It was not easy to think of Flora Hayes as being ashamed, but Sylvia felt quite sure that Flora felt sorry that she had attempted to deceive her friends.

"I knew it all the time," said Grace slowly, "and I told Sylvia it was you; didn't I, Sylvia?"

"Yes," said Sylvia, "and we knew you were sure to tell us about it, Flora. But you did look just like the picture of Lady Caroline."

Flora sat down. It had been so much easier to confess than she had expected. Neither Grace nor Sylvia had seemed resentful or surprised.

"You didn't tell me that you knew," she said, a little accusingly.

"Oh, well, we couldn't do that, Flora. You see we were your guests," Grace explained.

"And we knew you were sure to tell us," Sylvia added.

Flora was silent for a moment. She was thinking that both her friends had been rather fine about the whole affair. They had not run screaming from their room on the appearance of the "ghost," and alarmed the house, and so brought discovery and punishment and shame upon her; neither had they resented her not confessing.

"Well, I do think you two girls are the nicest girls in this town," she declared, "and I am mighty proud that you are my friends. I can tell you one thing: I'll never try to make anyone believe in ghosts again. I was half frightened to death myself when I crept up those stairs, and my shoulder has been lame ever since."

Grace and Sylvia had wondered what the large basket contained, but in their interest over Flora's beautiful gifts, and their delight in her "owning up" to being the "ghost," they had quite forgotten about it. It was Flora who now pointed at it and said laughingly: "I've brought my dolls in that basket."

"Molly and Polly will be glad enough to have company," Sylvia assured her.

Flora opened the basket and took out a large black "mammy" in a purple dress, white apron, and a yellow handkerchief twisted turban-fashion about her head.

"Mammy Jane always goes with the young ladies," she explained laughingly, and took out two fine china dolls dressed in white muslin with broad crimson silk sashes. Each of these fine ladies had a tiny parasol of crimson silk.

"I'm going home after my dolls," exclaimed Grace, and while Sylvia brought cushions for these unexpected visitors, and introduced them to Molly and Polly, Grace hurried home and was soon back again with her own treasured dolls, which she introduced as "Mr. and Mrs. and Miss Delaney."

The lesson in lace-making was quite forgotten as the three girls played with the array of dolls.

Sylvia ran to the door and called Estralla, who appeared so quickly that Sylvia wondered where she could have been. Estralla was told that she must help "Mammy Jane" take care of the doll visitors, and the little negro's face beamed with pleasure. Not one of the little girls in the pleasant room was as happy as Estralla; and when supper was ready and Sylvia and her friends went down-stairs, leaving Estralla in charge of all the dolls, she could hardly believe in her good fortune, and, as usual, was sure it was all due to her beloved Missy Sylvia.

After supper the dolls were all invited downstairs to be introduced to Sylvia's father and mother; and Estralla, smiling and delighted, was entrusted with bringing "Mammy Jane."

The three friends often looked back on that happy afternoon, for on the very next day Mr. Hayes decided to move his family to the plantation, and it was many days before Sylvia, Grace and Flora were to be together again. The citizens of Charleston, in December, 1860, were becoming anxious as to what might befall them. Very soon it might be possible that South Carolina would secede from the Union, and war with the northern states might follow. In such a ease the guns of Fort Sumter and Fort Moultrie might fire on Charleston, and many planters who had homes in Charleston were sending their families to their country homes. Northern men who had business in Charleston were also anxious, and Sylvia did not know that her own father was seriously considering a return to Boston.

But the little girls bade each other good-night with happy smiles and laughter, and without a thought but that they would have many more pleasant times together.

Sylvia did not even think of the lace-making until she brought down her pretty box to show to her mother and father.

"The Charleston people have been so kind to us," Mrs. Fulton said, a little sadly.

"They are the most courteous and kindly people in the world," declared Mr. Fulton.

Sylvia went up to her room wondering why her mother and father seemed so serious, when everything was so lovely. She had almost forgotten her adventure of the previous night, and went happily to bed with Flora's pretty gift on the light-stand beside her bed.

CHAPTER XIV

MR. ROBERT WAITE

I<small>T</small> was a very sober little darky who came up to Sylvia's room the next morning. She set down the pitcher of water and moved silently toward the door.

"What's the matter, Estralla?" Sylvia called; for usually Estralla was all smiles, and had a good deal to say.

Estralla shook her head. "Nuffin', Missy. I knowed you couldn't do nuffin' 'bout it. My mammy says how nobody can."

"Wait, Estralla! What do you mean?" exclaimed Sylvia, sitting up in bed.

"I'se gwine to be sold! Jes' like I tells you. My mammy was over to Massa Waite's house las' night, and she hears ober dar dat Massa Robert's gwine to sell off every nigger what ain't workin'—-this week!" Estralla's voice had drifted into her old-time wail.

"Oh, Estralla! What can I do?" and Sylvia was out of bed in a second, standing close beside the little colored girl.

"I dunno, Missy Sylvia. I 'spec' dar ain't nuffin' you kin do. But you has been mighty good to me," Estralla replied. "It's mighty hard to go off and leave my mammy an' never see you-all no more, Missy Sylvia. I dunno whar I'll be sent."

"Estralla, if you were earning wages for Mr. Robert Waite would he let you stay here?" Sylvia asked eagerly.

"I reckon he would, Missy. But who's a-gwine to pay wages for a pickaninny like me? Nobuddy! Missy, I'se a-gwine to run off an' hide myself 'til the Yankee soldiers comes and sets us free," said Estralla.

"You can't do that. But don't be frightened, Estralla. I have thought of something. I will hire you! Yes, I will; and pay wages for you to Mr. Waite. I'll go tell him so this very day," declared Sylvia, her face brightening, as she remembered the twenty dollars in gold which her Grandmother Fulton had given her when she had left Boston. "You can do whatever you please with it," was what Grandmother Fulton had said. Sylvia had thought that she would ask her mother to buy her a watch with the money, but she did not remember that now. She knew that, more than anything, she would rather keep Estralla safe. Twenty dollars was a good deal of money, she reflected. If the northern soldiers would only come quickly and set the slaves free! But even if they did not come for a long time the money would surely pay Mr. Waite wages for Estralla, so that he would not insist on selling her.

Estralla's face had brightened instantly at Sylvia's promise. And when Sylvia explained that she had money of her very own, and even opened her writing desk and showed Estralla the shining gold pieces, the little darky's fears vanished. She was as sure that all would be well now, as she had been frightened and despondent when she entered the room.

"Shall I tell my mammy?" she asked eagerly.

"Yes," Sylvia responded. "I know my mother will let me. Because Grandma said I could do as I pleased with the money. And I please to pay it to Mr. Waite."

"Then I'll be your maid, won't I, Missy Sylvia?" chuckled the little darky with proud delight, "an' I'll allers go whar yo' goes, like Missy Flora Hayes' mammy does."

"Why, yes, I suppose you will," agreed Sylvia.

Sylvia had meant to tell her mother and father of her plan about Estralla at breakfast time, but her father was just leaving the dining-room when she came in.

"Are you going to ask your little friends to go out in the *Butterfly* this afternoon?" he asked. "If you want to go to the forts you must be on hand early."

"I'll ask them right away after breakfast, before they start for school," Sylvia promised eagerly. She was glad that she could go to the forts again, and tell Mrs. Carleton that she had given the letter to Mr. Doane. This filled her thoughts for the moment, so she quite forgot about her plan to employ Estralla, especially as her mother had decided that lessons would not begin until the following week.

It had seemed to Mrs. Fulton that her little daughter was tired, and not as well as usual, and she was glad that the sailing expedition would take her out for a long afternoon on the water.

Sylvia ate her breakfast hurriedly, and ran up-stairs for her cape and hat, to find Estralla waiting just inside the door of her room.

"W'at yo' mammy say 'bout my bein' yo' maid?" questioned the little darky.

"Oh, it will be all right. I am going to ask Grace and Flora to go sailing this afternoon, and I'll keep on to Mr. Robert Waite's and have it all settled this morning," Sylvia replied, putting on her pretty new hat.

"You may come, too," she added.

"Yas, Missy. W'at yo' reckon Massa Robert gwine to say?" questioned Estralla earnestly.

"I think I will take the money," Sylvia said, not answering Estralla's question; "then Mr. Waite will be sure that I can pay him."

Mrs. Fulton saw Sylvia, closely followed by Estralla, running across the garden toward the house where Grace Waite lived.

"Poor little darky! What will she do when Sylvia goes north?" she thought. For Mr. Fulton had told her that very morning that he was sure South Carolina would secede from the Union, and then northern men would no longer be welcome in Charleston. That meant of course that the Fultons would have to return to Boston, if that were possible, but all communication with northern states might be prevented. It was no wonder that Mr. and Mrs. Fulton were anxious and worried.

Grace was ready to start for school when Sylvia and Estralla arrived, and her mother gave her consent at once for her to go sailing in the afternoon.

"The Christmas holidays will soon be here, so a half day out of school will not matter," Mrs. Waite said smilingly, and gave Grace a note for Miss Patten.

"I'll walk to Flora's with you," said Grace. "Now, Sylvia, own up that you think Charleston is nicer than Boston. Why, it is all ice and snow and cold weather up there, and here it is warm and pleasant. You couldn't go sailing if you were in Boston to-day," she added laughingly.

"No, but I could go sleighing," responded Sylvia.

As they came in sight of Flora's home they both exclaimed in surprise:

"Why, they are all going away! Look, Flora and her mother are in the carriage!" said Grace, "and there is Philip on horseback."

The carriage had turned on to the street, and even as Grace spoke a curve in the road hid it from view.

Philip, evidently giving some directions to the negroes who were loading trunks and boxes into a cart, rode down the driveway just as Grace and Sylvia reached the entrance.

He greeted them smilingly, and stopped his horse to speak with them.

"It was all planned for us to go to the plantation before Flora got home last night," he explained. "Father thought it was best for the family to be out of the city. You see, it's getting time for Carolinians to take possession of the forts, and there may be trouble. But the palmetto flag will soon float over Fort Sumter," he added smilingly, and with a touch of his cap and a smiling good-bye he rode off.

Sylvia was sorry that Flora was going away, but that Philip should want the palmetto flag to take the place of the Stars and Stripes over Fort Sumter seemed a much greater misfortune. "When he knows it stands for slavery," she thought, wondering if he had entirely forgotten about Dinkie.

"I'll have to run, or I'll be late for school," declared Grace. "I'll be all ready when you call," and with a gay good-bye she was off down the street, leaving Sylvia and Estralla standing alone near the high wall which enclosed the garden of the Hayes house.

"Massa Robert Waite, he live right 'roun' de corner," said Estralla, and the two girls turned down the street leading to the house of Estralla's master.

Sylvia went up the flight of stone steps which led to Mr. Waite's door a little fearfully. A tall, good-natured colored man opened the door and asked her errand, and then led the way across the wide hall and rapped at a door.

"A little white missy to see you, Massa Robert," he said, and in a moment Sylvia found herself standing before a smiling gentleman, whose red face and white whiskers made her think of the pictures of Santa Claus.

"Won't you be seated, young lady?" he said, very politely, waving his hand toward a low cushioned chair, and bowing "as if I were really grown up," thought Sylvia.

"I am Sylvia Fulton," she said, wondering why her voice sounded so faint.

"Perhaps you are the daughter of Mr. John Fulton, who does me the favor of renting my house on the East Battery," responded Mr. Waite, with another bow.

"Yes, sir," said Sylvia meekly, wondering whether she would ever dare tell him her errand. There was a little silence, and then Mr. Waite took a seat near his little visitor and said:

"Let me see; is not your name in a song? 'Then to Sylvia let us sing,'" he hummed, beating time with his right hand.

"Oh, yes, I was named for that song. And, if you please, Mr. Waite, would you let me pay you wages for Estralla?"

"For Estralla? Now, of course, I ought to know all about Estralla. But, you see, I have a man who attends to the names, and all that, of my negroes. But perhaps you can tell me who Estralla is?" replied Mr. Waite.

"If you please, sir, she is Aunt Connie's little girl, and she lives with us, and I like her, and I thought——" began Sylvia, but Mr. Waite raised his hand, and she stopped suddenly.

"I see! I see! You want her to wait upon you. I see. Quite right. But if she is living in your house she is not costing me a penny for board. So I am indebted to you. Well! Well! I must see that whatever you wish is carried out. You need not pay me wages, little Miss Sylvia, but you shall have the girl for your own servant as long as you live in my house, and I am delighted to have you take her off my hands. Yes, indeed! Yes, indeed!" and Mr. Waite smiled and bowed, and seemed exactly like Santa Claus.

"I'm ever so much obliged," said Sylvia. "I like Estralla."

"Do you? Yes! Well! And I hope you will come again, Miss Sylvia. I am greatly pleased to have made your acquaintance," and the polite gentleman escorted her to the door, where he bade her good-bye with such an elegant bow that Sylvia nearly fell backward in her effort to make as low a curtsey as seemed necessary.

Estralla had hidden herself behind some shrubbery, and joined Sylvia at the gate.

"Would he hire me out, Missy?" she asked eagerly.

"My, no!" answered Sylvia, and before she could explain the generosity of Estralla's owner, the little darky was wailing and sobbing: "I knowed I'd be sold! I knowed it."

"Keep still, Estralla! Mr. Waite says I may have you without paying him. Just as long as I live in his house he said you were to be my maid! Oh, Estralla! He was just as kind and polite as if I had been a grown-up young lady," said Sylvia with enthusiasm.

"Yas'm, I reckons he would hafter be, 'cos he's a Carolinian gen'man. I'se mighty glad he gives me to you, Missy. I reckon my mammy's gwine to be glad," and Estralla, quite forgetting that there was such a thing as trouble in the world, danced along beside her new mistress.

Sylvia hurried home, eager to tell her mother of her wonderful new friend, and of Flora's departure to the plantation.

Mrs. Fulton listened in surprise. But when Sylvia finished her story of Mr. Waite's kindness, declaring that he was just like Santa Claus, she did not reprove her for going on such an errand without permission, but agreed with her little daughter that Mr. Robert Waite was a very kind and generous gentleman.

Aunt Connie was as delighted as it was possible for a mother to be who knows that her youngest child is safe under the same roof with herself. She tried to thank

Sylvia for protecting Estralla, but Sylvia was too happy over her success to listen to her.

When Grace returned from school Sylvia ran over and told her all about her Uncle Robert's kindness.

Grace listened with wondering eyes.

"Oh, that's just like Uncle Robert," she declared. "But I think you were brave to ask him."

CHAPTER XV

THE *Butterfly* was all ready and waiting for its passengers when Grace and Sylvia, followed by the smiling and delighted Estralla, who was carrying Sylvia's cape and trying to act as much like a "rale grown-up lady's maid" as possible, came down to the long wharf.

Although it was December, there was little to remind anyone of winter. The air was soft and clear, the sun shone brightly, and only a little westerly breeze ruffled the blue waters of the harbor.

Negroes were at work on the wharf loading bales of cotton on a big ship. They were singing as they worked, and Sylvia resolved to remember the words of the song:

> "De big bee flies high,
> De little bee makes de honey,
> De black man raise de cotton,
> An' de white man gets de money."

She repeated it over and then Grace sang it, with an amused laugh at her friend's interest in "nigger songs."

Mr. Fulton came to meet them and helped them on board the boat. As the *Butterfly* made its way out into the channel the little girls looked back at the long water-front, where lay many vessels from far-off ports. In the distance they could see the spire of St. Philip's, one of the historic churches of Charleston, and everywhere fluttered the palmetto flag.

Sylvia sat in the stern beside her father, and very soon the tiller was in her hand and she was shaping the boat's course toward the forts. Grace watched her admiringly.

"I believe you could steer in the dark," she declared.

"Of course she could if she had a compass and was familiar with the stars," said Mr. Fulton; and he called Grace's attention to the compass fastened securely near Sylvia's seat, and explained the rules of navigation.

"Is that the way the big ships know how to find their harbors?" asked Grace, when Mr. Fulton told her of the stars, and bow the pilots set their course.

"Yes, and if Sylvia understood how to steer by the compass she could steer the *Butterfly* as well at night as she can now."

Sylvia looked at the compass with a new interest; she was sure that navigation would be a much more interesting study than grammar, and resolved to ask her father to teach her how to "box the compass."

There had been many changes at Fort Moultrie since Sylvia's last visit. A deep ditch had been dug between the fort and the sand-bars, and many workmen were

"I BELIEVE YOU COULD STEER IN THE DARK"

busy in strengthening the defences, and Sylvia and Grace wondered why so many soldiers were stationed along the parapet.

Captain Carleton seemed very glad to welcome them, and sent a soldier to escort the girls to the officers' quarters, while Mr. Fulton went in search of Major Anderson. Sylvia wondered if she would have a chance to tell Mrs. Carleton that she had safely delivered the message.

Mrs. Carleton was in her pleasant sitting-room and declared that she had been wishing for company, and held up some strips of red and white bunting. "I am making a new flag for Fort Sumter," she said. "Perhaps you will help me sew on the stars, one for each State, you know."

"Is there one for South Carolina?" asked Grace, as Mrs. Carleton found two small thimbles, which she said she had used when she was no older than Sylvia, and showed the girls how to sew the white stars securely on the blue.

"Yes, indeed! One of the first stars on the flag was for South Carolina," replied Mrs. Carleton, "and this very fort was named for a defender of America's rights."

While Grace and Sylvia were so pleasantly occupied Estralla had wandered out, crossed the bridge which connected the officers' quarters with the fort, and now found herself near the landing-place, so that when Mrs. Carleton made the girls a cup of hot chocolate and

looked about to give Estralla her share, the little colored girl was not to be seen.

"I'll call her," said Sylvia, and ran out on the veranda.

No response came to her calls, so she went down the
steps and along the walk which led to the sand-bars,
past the houses and barracks on Sullivan's Island. No
one was in sight whom she could ask if Estralla had
passed that way. She climbed a small sand-hill covered
with stunted little trees and looked about, but could
see no trace of the little darky. It had not occurred to
Sylvia that Estralla would go back to the fort.

"Oh, dear! I wonder where she can be," thought
Sylvia, calling "Estralla! Estralla!" and sure that if she
was within hearing Estralla would instantly appear. As
Sylvia climbed over the sandy slope she saw here and
there a small green vine with glossy leaves and a tiny
yellow blossom, and resolved to gather a bunch to
carry back to Mrs. Carleton. "When I give them to her
I'll have a chance to say that Mr. Doane has the letter,"
she thought.

Wandering on in search of the flowers, she went further and further from the fort, up one sand slope and
down another, almost forgetting her search for Estralla, and finally deciding that it was time to go back to
Mrs. Carleton.

"Probably Estralla is there before this, and they will
be looking for me," she thought, and climbed another
sandy slope, expecting to see the houses and barracks

directly in front of her. But she found herself facing the open sea, and look which way she would there was only shore, sand heaps and blue water.

But Sylvia was not at all alarmed. She was sure that all she had to do was to follow the line of shore and she would soon be in sight of some familiar place, so she started singing to herself as she walked on:

> "De big bee files high,
>   De little bee makes de honey,"

and hoping that Mrs. Carleton would not think that she had been careless in losing her way.

It was rather difficult walking. Her feet slipped in the sand, and after a little Sylvia decided not to follow the shore, but to climb back over the sand-hills.

A cold wind was now blowing from the water, and she was glad of the shelter of the stunted trees, and decided to rest for a little while.

"Of course I can't be lost, because I know exactly where I am. This is Sullivan's Island, and the fort is right over there. I mustn't rest but a minute, for my father said we would start home early," she thought, and again started on, going directly away from the fort, and over sand-hills and into little sloping valleys farther and farther away from familiar places.

The December day drew to a close, and dusky shadows crept over the island. Once or twice Sylvia's wanderings had brought her back to the shore, but not until the darkness began to gather did she really understand that she was lost, and that she was too tired to walk much longer. She thought of the little compass on board the *Butterfly*, and wondered if a compass would help anyone find her way on land as well as on the sea. At last she began to call aloud: "Estralla! Estralla!" feeling almost sure that, like herself, Estralla must be wandering about lost in the sand-hills.

It was nearly dark before she gave up trying to find her way to the fort, and, shivering and half afraid, crawled under the scraggly branches of some stunted trees on a sheltered slope.

"My father will come and find me, I know he will," she said aloud, almost ready to cry. "I'll wait here, and keep calling 'Estralla,' so he will hear me."

A few moments after Sylvia started to find Estralla Mrs. Carleton had been called to a neighbor's house. "Tell Sylvia I won't be gone long," she had said to Grace.

Grace did not mind being alone until Sylvia returned. She helped herself to the rich creamy chocolate and the little frosted cakes, and then curled up on a broad couch near the window with a book full of wonderful pictures. The pictures were of a tall man on horseback, and a short, fat man on a donkey. "The Adventures of Don Quixote," was the title of the book, and after

Grace began to read she entirely forgot Sylvia, Estralla, and Mrs. Carleton. And not until Mr. Fulton came into the room an hour later did she lift her eyes from the book.

"All ready to start!" said Mr. Fulton, "and it will be dusk before we reach home. Where is Sylvia?"

"Oh!" exclaimed Grace, looking up in surprise. "Hasn't she come back with Estralla? Mrs. Carleton has just gone to the next house."

"Well, put on your things and run after them, that's a good girl," said Mr. Fulton. "Why, here is Estralla now," he added, as the little colored girl appeared at the door. "Tell Miss Sylvia to come down to the landing; I'll meet you there," and he hurried away, thinking his little daughter was safe with Mrs. Carleton.

"Whar' is Missy Sylvia?" asked Estralla, who had been asleep in a sunny corner of the veranda for the last hour.

"Where is Sylvia?" echoed Mrs. Carleton, who came in at that moment. "Has she gone to the boat?"

"Why, I don't know. Perhaps she has. Mr. Fulton said for us to come right to the landing," said Grace, her thoughts still full of the faithful Sancho Panza of whom she had been reading.

"I will go to the wharf with you. It was too bad to leave you. I must see Sylvia before she goes. Perhaps I may not be permitted to have visitors much longer," said Mrs. Carleton, and she and Grace left the pleasant room and, followed closely by Estralla, made their way over the bridge to the landing-place.

"Where is Sylvia?" asked Mr. Fulton, looking at his watch. "We really ought to have started an hour ago.

For a moment the little group looked at each other in silence. Then with a sudden cry Estralla darted off.

Mrs. Carleton hurriedly explained Sylvia's starting off to find Estralla, and her own departure. She blamed herself that she had permitted Sylvia to go out alone.

"She must be somewhere about the fort," declared Captain Carleton.

"Oh, yes," agreed Mr. Fulton, "but we had best lose no time in finding her."

While Captain Carleton questioned the soldiers, Mr. Fulton and Mrs. Carleton and Grace hastened back to the officers' quarters, and a thorough search for the little girl was begun at once. No one gave a thought to Estralla, who had traced her little mistress along the street, and was now running along a sandy slope beyond the barracks calling: "Missy Sylvia! Missy Sylvia!" But no answer came to her calls.

CHAPTER XVI

IN DANGER

Estralla did not know why she was so sure that Missy Sylvia had wandered out beyond the barracks; but, since her little mistress was not at Mrs. Carleton's, and had not come to the landing-place, the little colored girl was sure that she must be among the sand-hills, and she ran along calling Sylvia's name as she ran.

Now and then she stopped to listen for some response, or to look about for some sign that might tell her that Sylvia had passed that way, and near the top of one of the little slopes she found a bunch of the green vines and yellow blossoms which Sylvia had dropped.

"She shuah am somewhar near," thought Estralla, and just then she heard a far-off call.

"Dat was my name!" she exclaimed aloud, and listened more intently than ever.

"Maybe 'twas jes' one o' them gull-birds a-callin'," she decided as no further sound came to her ears.

Now she went on more carefully, but she, too, came to the shore; but it was on the inner curve of the land, a little cove where an old shanty stood near the water, and a boat was drawn up near by.

Estralla looked into the rough cabin, half hoping to find Sylvia there. Then she went back a little way and shouted Sylvia's name again and again, and this time there was a response.

"Estralla! Estralla!" came clearly to her ears.

My lan' o' grashus!" whispered the little darky, and then called loudly, "I'se a-comin', Missy Sylvia." And now Sylvia called again. Back and forth sounded the voices of the two girls, each one moving toward the other, for at the welcome sound of Estralla's call Sylvia had sprung up and hurried in the direction from which the voice seemed to come.

It was now so nearly dusk that as they came in sight of each other they were like dark shadows.

"Oh, Estralla! Where is my father?" Sylvia cried as Estralla ran toward her and flung both arms about her little mistress.

"He's a-waitin' fer yo', Missy! Don' be skeered; I'se gwine to take keer of yo'."

"Do you know the way back, Estralla?" asked Sylvia. "I couldn't find the fort."

"No, Missy; I reckon we couldn't fin' nuthin' now, 'tis too nigh dark. But thar's a cabin an' a boat jes' over t'other side o' dis san' heap. I kin fin' them," responded Estralla, turning back. They walked very slowly, for Estralla wanted to be quite sure that they were going in the right direction, and not until they were in sight of the cabin and the shadowy outlines of the boat did she feel safe. Then with a sigh of relief she exclaimed:

"W'at I tell yo', Missy Sylvia! Ain't dar a boat, like what I said? An' don' yo' know all 'bout a boat? Course yo' does. Now yo' can sail us right off home. An' when yo' pa comes home 'mos' skeered to def, 'cos he cyan't fin' yo', thar' yo'll be," and Estralla chuckled happily as if all their troubles were over.

But Sylvia was not so sure. Unless there was a sail or a pair of oars the boat would be of little use, and even with oars and sail could she guide the boat safely to Charleston?

They soon discovered that there was a pair of oars in the boat, but there was no sail or tiller. Sylvia could row, but Estralla could not be of any use. But it seemed the only way in which they could reach either Fort Moultrie or their house, for both the little girls realized that they might wander about the sand-hills all night without finding their way back to the fort. It was chilly and dark, and the old cabin with its sagging roof and open doorway was not a very inviting shelter. Indeed, Estralla was quite sure that a lion, or at the very least a family of wolves, was at that moment safely hidden in one of the dark corners of the cabin.

"The moon is out! Look!" said Sylvia, "and there goes a steamer."

Sylvia did not know that this steamer was a guard-
boat which Governor Pickens of South Carolina had
ordered stationed between Sullivan's Island and Fort
Sumter to prevent, if possible, any United States troops
being landed at that fort.

"I can see the fort!" declared Sylvia. "That's it off
beyond the boat," and she pointed down the harbor.
"Now, we will start. I know I can row the boat that far,
and I am sure my father will not go home without us.
Tomorrow we will send this boat back."

Sylvia had now forgotten all her weariness, and she
was no longer afraid. She was sure that in a little while
she would be safely at the fort, and then, she resolved,
she would at once tell Mrs. Carleton that Mr. Doane
had the letter and ask permission to tell her mother of
her part in the secret message.

The boat was already half afloat, and it was an easy
matter to pull up the big stone attached to a strong
rope which served as an anchor, and then to push off
from shore.

"You watch, Estralla, and if any other boat comes near
shout at the top of your voice," said Sylvia as she dipped
the oars into the dark water and pulled off from shore.

"My lan', Missy! Dar's dat light agin," called the half-
frightened darky, "an' we's right in it dis time!

An instant later a call came from the guard-boat.
"Boat ahoy! Where bound?" and before Sylvia could

ship her oars or answer the call she found herself looking straight into the blinding light, and felt the little boat
rising on the crest of the wave made by the steamer.

"We's gwine to be drownded, Missy!" shouted
Estralla, and before Sylvia could say a word the frightened little darky had sprung up and lurched forward
across Sylvia's knees.

The boat tipped and the water rushed over one side,
but Sylvia, clutching the oars steadily, and remembering her father's frequent warnings, sat perfectly still
and the little craft righted itself.

"You nearly upset us; keep still where you are.
Don't move!" said Sylvia angrily. The light had
flashed in another direction now, and the guard-
boat had moved on, thinking the boat contained two
young darkies bound for Sullivan's Island after a visit
to Charleston.

Sylvia could feel the water about her feet and ankles.
She wished that she had called for help, for she realized
now that they might be run into and sunk by some
passing craft. Beside that the wind and tide were now
carrying them swiftly along toward the open sea. Then,
suddenly, Sylvia dropped her oars and screamed at the
top of her voice. Estralla shouted loudly. Their boat
had run directly against the wall of Fort Sumter. In an
instant there were lights flashing over the parapet.
There was the sound of voices, a call, and then the lit-

tle craft was held firmly against the barricade and a gruff voice called:

"Stop your noise, and we'll have you safe in a jiffy."

But it seemed a long time to the frightened children before a tall soldier swung over into the boat and lifted Sylvia and then Estralla up to the outstretched hands which grasped them so firmly.

"What on earth were you out in that boat for?" questioned an elderly gruff-voiced officer, when Sylvia and Estralla, thoroughly drenched and wondering what new misfortune was in store for them, followed him into a bare little cell-like room where the lamplight made them blink and shield their eyes for a moment.

Sylvia told of their adventures as quickly as possible, and the officer listened in amazement.

"Upon my word!" he said as she finished. "It's a wonder you are alive to tell the story. And so you are a little Yankee girl? Well! Come along to my quarters and my wife will put you both to bed, or you'll be too ill to go home to-morrow."

"Can't we go to Fort Moultrie right away?" pleaded Sylvia. "My father must be worried about me."

"No one from this fort can go to Fort Moultrie," he responded gravely. "Those flash-lights are from a guard-boat which the South Carolina people have sent down the harbor so that Major Anderson won't send us reinforcements without their knowledge. I wish Anderson would send some message to the President," he added, as if thinking aloud.

Sylvia wondered to herself if the letter she had carried to Mr. Doane might not be a message to the President? She wished she could tell this big officer about it. But she remembered her promise to Mrs. Carleton not to speak of it to anyone.

"Here's a half-drowned little Yankee girl and her little darky," said the officer, as he led the two girls into a warm pleasant room where a pretty elderly lady with white hair sat with her needlework.

"For pity sake, Gerald!" she exclaimed. "They are shivering with cold," and without asking a single question she began to take off Sylvia's wet dress.

"Gerald, send Sally right in with hot milk," she directed, and the officer vanished.

It was not long before Sylvia was sitting up in bed wrapped in a gay-colored blanket and drinking milk so hot and sweet and spicy that it seemed as if she could never have enough of it. Estralla was curled up in a big scarlet wrapper on a rug near the fire with a big mug of the spiced and sweetened milk. And when they had finished this a plate of hot buttered biscuit, and thin slices of ham, was brought in. Then there was more warm milk.

"Now you must both go straight to sleep," commanded Mrs. Gerald," and to-morrow morning my husband will take you safely home," and kissing Sylvia, and with a kindly smile for Estralla, the friendly woman bade them good-night.

There was no light now in the room save the dancing firelight. Sylvia lay watching the shadows on the wall. Estralla was fast asleep, but her little mistress lay awake thinking over the adventures of the day. She was at Fort Sumter, the long dark fort which she had so often seen with the Stars and Stripes waving above it from her home, from Miss Patten's schoolroom, and in her sails about the harbor. Sylvia snuggled down in her comfortable bed with a sense of safety and comfort. "I wish my father and mother could know I am at Fort Sumter," was her last waking thought.

CHAPTER XVII

A CHRISTMAS PRESENT

EVERY nook and corner of Fort Moultrie was searched for the missing Sylvia, and when no trace of her could be discovered, her friends became nearly certain that the little girl must have slipped from the landing-place into the sea, and that it was useless to search for her. But it was late in the evening before Mr. Fulton gave up the search, and with a sad and anxious heart headed the *Butterfly* toward Charleston. He still hoped that his little girl might be found. A party of soldiers, headed by Captain Carleton, had started to search for her on Sullivan's Island, but this had not been determined upon until late in the evening, at about the time when Estralla and Sylvia were embarking upon their adventurous voyage to Fort Sumter.

No one had given a thought to the little darky girl. She was supposed to be somewhere about the fort.

Grace, warmly wrapped in a thick shawl, sat beside Mr. Fulton as the *Butterfly* made its swift way across the dark harbor. They could see the dark line of the guard-boat, but they were not molested and came into the wharf safely. Grace held close to Mr. Fulton's hand as they hurried toward home with the sad news of Sylvia's disappearance. Neither of them spoke until they reached the walk leading to the door of Grace's home, then Grace said:

"I know Sylvia will be found. Estralla will surely find her and bring her hone."

"Estralla! Why, I had entirely forgotten her," responded Mr. Fulton.

"She ran off as soon as Sylvia was missed," Grace continued earnestly, "and she will find her. Probably she has found her before this."

"I believe you are right. Estralla is a clever little darky, and if she started in search of Sylvia perhaps she has been able to find her. I had not thought of it," and Mr. Fulton's voice had a new note of hope.

"Thank you, Grace. I will start back to the fort as soon as I have talked with Sylvia's mother."

But on Mr. Fulton's return to the wharf he found a sentry on guard who refused him permission to go to the fort. It was in vain that Mr. Fulton explained that his little daughter was lost, that he must be permitted to return to the fort.

The sentry wasted no words. "Orders, sir. Sorry," was the only response he could get, and at midnight Mr. Fulton was in his own house looking out over the harbor. Mingled with his anxious fear for the safety of his little daughter was the thought of the sentries now guarding Charleston's water-front, of the assembling of soldiers in the city, and the evident plan of the southerners to seize the forts in the harbor and force the Government into war.

He realized that in that case it would not be possible for his family to remain in Charleston.

Early the next morning Sylvia was awakened and made ready for her return, and when the sun shone brightly over the waters of the harbor she and Estralla, with Captain Gerald and a strong negro servant, were on board a boat sailing rapidly toward home.

They landed at the wharf where the *Butterfly* was fastened, and before Captain Gerald had stepped on shore Sylvia called out: "Father! Father! There he is! And Mother, too!" and in another moment her mother's arms were about her, and she was telling as rapidly as possible the story of her adventures, and of Estralla coming to her rescue.

Grace came running to meet Sylvia as they came near their home.

"Oh, Sylvia, I wish I had been with you," she exclaimed. "That is twice you have been to Fort Sumter without meaning to go, isn't it?"

"We will hope that her next visit will not be as dangerous as this one," said Mr. Fulton soberly.

For several days Sylvia could think and talk only of her wanderings among the sand-hills, and of her first

sight of the guard-boat. She began teaching Estralla
on the very day of her return, and the little darky made
rapid progress.

"Father, when may we go to Fort Moultrie again?"
she asked one morning a few days later, for she wanted very much to see Mrs. Carleton, and was quite sure
that her father would be ready to sail down the harbor on any pleasant day, and his reply made her look
up in surprise.

"I do not know that we shall ever go to the forts
again," her father had replied. "Did you not hear the
bells ringing and the military music yesterday? South
Carolina has seceded from the Union. No one is allowed
to go to the forts. And unless Major Anderson takes possession of Fort Sumter the Confederates will."

"And we are to start for Boston next week, dear
child," Sylvia's mother added.

It seemed to Sylvia that her mother was very glad
at the thought of returning to her former home. But
Sylvia was not glad. What would become of Estralla?

Mr. Waite had said that as long as Sylvia lived in his
house the little colored girl could be her maid. But if
they went to Boston and left Estralla behind Sylvia was
sure that there would be nothing but trouble for the
faithful little darky.

"Why, Sylvia! What is the matter?" questioned her
mother anxiously; for Sylvia was leaning her head on
the table.

"I can't go to Boston and leave Estralla!" she sobbed. "She has done lots of brave things for me. She wouldn't leave me to be a slave."

Mr. and Mrs. Fulton looked at each other with puzzled eyes.

"But Estralla would not want to leave her mammy," suggested Mr. Fulton.

"Oh, Father! Can't Aunt Connie and Estralla go with us?" and Sylvia lifted her head and looked hopefully at her father. "Couldn't I buy Estralla and then make her free? I've got that gold money Grandma gave me."

"I am afraid it wouldn't be much use for me to even try to buy a slave's freedom now," Mr. Fulton said a little sadly. "Don't suggest such a thing to Aunt Connie, Sylvia."

"When shall we go to Boston?" Sylvia asked.

"Right away after Christmas, unless Fort Sumter is attacked before that time. Washington ought to send troops and provisions for the forts at once!" replied Mr. Fulton.

After her father had left the house Sylvia and her mother went up to Mrs. Fulton's pleasant sitting-room.

"We must begin to pack at once," declared Sylvia's mother, "and do not go outside the gate alone, Sylvia. I wish we could leave Charleston immediately."

"Won't I see Mrs. Carleton again?" Sylvia asked anxiously.

"I do not know, dear child. But run away and give Estralla her lesson, as usual. It will not be a very gay Christmas for any of us this year," responded Mrs. Fulton, and Sylvia went slowly to her own room where Estralla was waiting for her.

The little colored girl had put the room in order; there was a bright fire in the grate, the morning sunshine filled the room, and Miss Molly and Polly, smiling as usual, were in the tiny chairs behind the little round table.

"Dar's gwine to be war, Missy!" Estralla declared solemnly. "Yas'm. Dar's soldiers comin' in from ebery place. Won't de Yankees come and set us free, Missy?"

Sylvia shook her head. "I don't know, Estralla! Let's not talk about it," she replied.

"Wal, Missy, lots of darkies are runnin' off! My mammy say we'll stay right here 'til Massa Fulton goes, an' den"—Estralla stopped, leaned a little nearer to Sylvia and whispered, "an' *den* my mammy an' I we'se gwine to go with Massa Fulton."

Mrs. Fulton was not in her room, so Sylvia went down the stairs to look for her. She heard voices in the sitting-room, and turned in that direction.

"Oh!" she whispered, as she stood in the open door. For her mother was sitting on the big sofa near the open fire, and beside her sat Mr. Robert Waite, while her father was standing in front of them. They were all talking so earnestly that they did not notice the surprised little girl standing in the doorway, and Sylvia heard Mr. Waite say:

"I shall be glad to protect your interests here, Mr. Fulton, as far as it is possible to do so. And you had better leave Charleston immediately. The city is no longer a safe place for northern people. The conflict may begin at any moment."

"'Conflict,'" Sylvia repeated the word to herself. Probably it meant something dreadful, she thought, recalling the "question period" at Miss Rosalie's school.

Just then Mr. Waite glanced toward the door and saw Sylvia. In a second he was on his feet, bowing as politely as on their last meeting.

"Miss Sylvia, I am glad to see you again," and he stepped forward to meet her.

Sylvia, feeling quite grown-up, made her pretty curtsey, and smiled with delight at Mr. Waite's greeting, as he led her toward her mother and, with another polite bow, gave her the seat on the sofa.

"I was hoping to see Miss Sylvia," he said. "I had meant to make her a little Christmas gift, with your permission," and he bowed again to Mrs. Fulton. "She was kind enough to interest herself in behalf of one of my people, the little darky, Estralla. And so I thought this would please you," and he smiled at Sylvia, who began to be sure that Mr. Waite and

Santa Claus must be exactly alike. As he spoke he handed Sylvia a long envelope.

"Do not open it until to-morrow, if you please," he added.

Sylvia promised and thanked him. She wondered if the envelope might not contain a picture of this kind friend. She knew that she must not ask a question; questions were never polite, she remembered, especially about a gift. But whatever it was she was very happy to think Mr. Robert Waite had remembered her.

They all went to the door with their friendly visitor, and stood there until he had reached the gate. Then Sylvia said, speaking very slowly:

"I think Mr. Robert Waite is just like the Knights in that book, 'The Age of Chivalry.' They always did exactly what was right, and so does he; and they were polite and so is he."

"Then, my dear, perhaps you will always remember that to do brave and gentle deeds with kindness is what 'chivalry' means," responded Mrs. Fulton.

Grace came in that afternoon greatly excited that it was a holiday. The whole city was rejoicing over the fact that South Carolina had been the first of the southern states to secede from the Union. Palmetto flags floated everywhere; the streets were filled with marching men. Major Anderson in Fort Moultrie watched Fort Sumter with anxious eyes, hoping for a word from

Washington which would give him authority to occupy it before the Charleston men could turn its guns against him. Already Mr. Doane had reached Washington; the message Sylvia had carried through the night had been delivered, and its answer, by a trusted messenger, was on its way south.

CHAPTER XVIII

GREAT NEWS

SYLVIA carried the long envelope which Mr. Robert Waite had given her to her room, and put it in the drawer of her desk with the treasured gold pieces.

"It will be splendid to have a picture of Mr. Waite to show Grandma Fulton," she thought happily, "and I can tell her all about him."

Then her thoughts rested on Flora, in the "haunted house," and she opened the silk-covered work-box and tried on the pretty gold thimble. She thought of her gold pieces, and a sudden resolve came into her mind:

"I will give Flora and Grace each a gold locket, with my picture in it." And just then Mrs. Fulton entered the room, and Sylvia ran toward her:

"Mother! Mother! I have a beautiful plan. I want to give Flora and Grace each a present. I want to give them each a gold locket with my picture in it. On Grace's locket I want 'Grace from Sylvia,' and on Flora's, 'Flora from Sylvia.' I can pay for them with my gold money. I may, mayn't I, Mother?" and Sylvia looked eagerly toward her mother.

"Of course you may; but it is too late to get the pictures and lockets in time for Christmas," responded Mrs. Fulton.

"I don't care when; only if we do go back to Boston I want them to have something to remember me by," said Sylvia, remembering the unfailing loyalty of her two little southern friends.

"The day after Christmas we will select the lockets, and see about the pictures," said Mrs. Fulton. Before Sylvia could answer there came a tap at the door, and Aunt Connie, evidently rather anxious and uncertain, whispered:

"Dar's a lady, Mistress, a lady f'um de fort, an' she say——"

"It must be Mrs. Carleton. I'll go right down," responded Mrs. Fulton, and, followed by Sylvia, she hurried down the stairs, to find Mrs. Carleton awaiting them.

"Captain Carleton insisted that I should come to you," she said. "He feels sure that the Charleston men mean to take Fort Sumter at once. Major Anderson is sending the women and children away from Fort Moultrie to places of safety."

"Of course you must stay with us, and we are delighted to have you," said Mrs. Fulton. "We want to stay in Charleston unless it becomes necessary for us to leave."

Mrs. Carleton greeted Sylvia warmly, and, greatly to her surprise, said:

"I have not had the opportunity to thank you, dear child, for delivering the message safely. We have heard that Mr. Doane has presented the letter to the President, and Major Anderson is sure that reinforcements and provisions for the forts will be sent at once." Then turning to Mrs. Fulton, she continued: "I know this loyal child kept her secret, and that even you and her father do not realize what a service your little daughter has rendered to the cause of Freedom!"

Mrs. Fulton was looking at her visitor in amazement.

"Sylvia! Message! Secret?" she exclaimed in such a puzzled tone that both Mrs. Carleton and Sylvia laughed aloud.

"Tell her, Sylvia! And I want to hear how you delivered the letter," said Mrs. Carleton.

So Sylvia told the story of creeping out of the house at nearly midnight, of the man who had declared her to be a runaway darky, of Estralla following her, and of their return. "And the door was closed and fastened, although I left it open," she concluded.

Mrs. Fulton recalled that one night they had been slightly disturbed by some unusual noise and that Mr. Fulton had gone down-stairs and discovered the front door open. "And we blamed Aunt Connie," she added.

"I did want to tell you, Mother," said Sylvia, "but it's even better to have Mrs. Carleton tell you."

That evening the story was retold to Mr. Fulton, who listened with even more surprise than Sylvia's mother had shown. He said that Estralla had been as brave as Sylvia, and that he wished he could do an equal service for the United States.

"This will be a fine story to tell Grandma Fulton," he whispered to Sylvia, when he gave her his good-night kiss.

She awoke early, before Estralla appeared with the usual pitcher of hot water and to light the fire in the grate, and in a moment was out of bed and at her desk. She opened the envelope very carefully, expecting to see the pictured face of her kind friend smiling at her. But there was no picture. There were only two documents tied with red tape, and with big red seals on them, and a number of printed and signed papers.

"Oh, dear! It isn't anything at all except letters," exclaimed Sylvia, nearly ready to cry with disappointment. And, suddenly, she did cry— a cry so like Estralla's wail that the little darky just entering the room stopped short, and nearly dropped the pitcher of hot water.

"W'at's de matter, Missy? W'at *is* de matter?" Estralla demanded.

Tears were in Sylvia's eyes as she turned toward the little darky. They were not tears for her own disappointment at not finding the expected picture, but they were tears for what Sylvia believed to be the most bitter misfortune that could befall Estralla and Aunt

Connie. For she was sure that the papers in that envelope were to tell her that Aunt Connie and Estralla had both been sold. But she resolved quickly that Estralla should not know of this until she had told her mother.

"Nothing I can tell you now, Estralla," she said, wiping away her tears.

Estralla looked quite ready to weep with her young mistress, but she lit the fire, and crept silently out of the room.

Sylvia dressed as quickly as possible, picked up the papers and ran to her mother's room.

"Look, Mother! It's dreadful. It wasn't a picture of Mr. Robert Waite at all. It's just a lot of papers about Estralla and Aunt Connie being sold," and Sylvia began to cry bitterly.

Mr. Fulton took the papers and looked them over, while Sylvia with her mother's arm about her sobbed out her disappointment.

"Sold! Estralla! Why, my dear Sylvia, these papers give Aunt Connie and Estralla their freedom, from yesterday. And these," and Mr. Fulton held up the smaller documents, "give them permission to leave Charleston for the north at any time within six months."

For a moment neither Sylvia nor her mother made any response to this wonderful statement.

"Truly, Father? Truly?" exclaimed Sylvia with shining eyes.

"Yes. These papers have been recorded. Estralla and her mother are no longer slaves. They are free," said Mr. Fulton, as he folded the papers. "Mr. Waite has made you the finest gift in the world, little daughter," he added seriously.

"And Estralla and Aunt Connie may go to Boston with us?" pleaded Sylvia, quite sure that her father and mother would agree. "Won't Grandma be surprised to see them?"

Mrs. Carleton was as pleased and surprised as Sylvia herself over Mr. Waite's gift, and it was decided that directly after breakfast Sylvia should tell Aunt Connie and Estralla the wonderful news. It was too great to be kept a secret even until Christmas Day.

"Dar, Mammy! W'at I tells yo'? I tells yo' Missy Sylvia gwine to look out fer us," Estralla declared triumphantly, evidently not at all surprised.

"But it is Mr. Robert Waite who has given you your freedom," Sylvia reminded them, "and my father says that you must both go with me and thank him."

"Yas, Missy," responded Aunt Connie, "but I reckons we wouldn't be thankin' him if 'twan't fer yo'. Massa Robert *he* knows dat all his niggers gwine to be free jes' as soon as de Yankees come. Yas, indeedy, he knows. But we shuahly go long wid yo', Missy, an' thanks him. We knows our manners.

Many eyes turned to watch the smiling colored woman and the delighted little negro girl who walked down King Street that afternoon, one on each side of a little white girl who looked as well pleased as her companions, for Sylvia decided that no time should be lost in telling Mr. Robert Waite of how greatly his generosity was appreciated.

He welcomed Sylvia with his usual cordiality, and told Aunt Connie that he wished her good fortune, and sent her and Estralla home.

"I will walk back with your young mistress," he said, and Sylvia felt that it was the proudest day of her life when she walked up King Street beside the friendly southerner.

"He talks just as if I were grown up," thought Sylvia gratefully, when Mr. Waite spoke of the forts, and of the possibilities of war between the northern and southern states.

"Tell your father not to hasten his preparations to leave Charleston; you are among friends, and these difficulties may be adjusted," Mr. Waite said as he bade Sylvia good-bye, and wished her a happy Christmas.

CHAPTER XIX

SYLVIA MAKES A PROMISE

"It doesn't seem a bit like Christmas," declared Sylvia, as she stood at the sitting-room window looking out at the falling rain.

Christmas day of 1860 was a gloomy, rainy day in Charleston, and many people felt exactly as Sylvia did, that it was not like Christmas.

Grace came over in the morning bringing a little chased gold ring for Sylvia, which the little girl promised always to wear. She wished that she could tell Grace about the lockets, but decided it would be better to surprise Grace with the locket itself.

As soon as Grace returned home Sylvia ran to find her mother.

"We will go down street and buy the lockets to-morrow morning, won't we, Mother?" she asked, and Mrs. Fulton promised that they would start early.

Sylvia resolved that, if the lockets and pictures did not take all her money, she would buy a doll for Estralla. She knew that nothing else would please the little colored girl as much as a "truly" doll.

But the morning of December twenty-sixth found the city of Charleston angry and excited. Crowds collected in the streets, and Mr. Fulton received a message from Mr. Robert Waite asking him to remain at home until Mr. Waite arrived.

"What is the matter, Father?" Sylvia asked. "He isn't coming to take back Estralla, is he?"

"No, of course not, child. It is trouble over the forts," responded her father. And in a short time Mr. Waite arrived. But he was not smiling this morning. He was very grave and serious.

"Major Anderson has evacuated Moultrie, and he and his men are at Fort Sumter," said Mr. Waite. "I came to assure you that whatever action Charleston takes that I will protect your household and property as far as possible."

Then Sylvia heard him say that Governor Pickens had seized Castle Pinckney, and that troops had been sent to Sullivan's Island to occupy Fort Moultrie, and the United States Arsenal, situated in the midst of the city of Charleston, was also in possession of the secessionists.

Sylvia listened to every word, but without much idea of what it all meant.

"Can't we buy the lockets to-day, Mother?" she asked.

"No, we must not go on the streets to-day," Mrs. Fulton answered; but Mr. Waite smiled at the little girl and said:

"I will gladly accompany Miss Sylvia if she has errands to do," so Sylvia told him about the pictures and lockets for Grace and Flora, and Mr. Waite assured her mother and father that he could easily spare the time to go with her upon so pleasant an errand. The friendly man realized that the little household were troubled and anxious, and that it would reassure them if their little girl could safely carry out her plan. So the two set forth together.

Mr. Robert Waite was too well known for any southerner to doubt his loyalty to South Carolina, and his visit to Mr. Fulton's house was in itself a protection to the family. As they walked along Sylvia told him how kind Grace and Flora had been to her.

"If we should go away the lockets will remind them how much I think of them," she said, and Mr. Waite smiled and said: "Yes, indeed," but it seemed to Sylvia that he was not really thinking about the lockets.

She held close to his hand, for there were crowds on every corner, and loud and violent threats against Major Anderson were heard from nearly every group. Sylvia heard one man declare that it was the duty of Charleston men to fire upon Fort Sumter at once; and before they reached the shop where she was to purchase the lockets Sylvia began to fear that she would never see Captain Carleton again.

The lockets were purchased, and Mr. Waite took Sylvia to a studio to sit for the pictures for the lockets. There

was enough money left to purchase a fine doll for Estralla, and Mr. Waite gave her a box filled with candy of many
kinds, shapes and flavors. All these things occupied her
thoughts so pleasantly that for a time she quite forgot
the disturbance in the streets, and all the trouble that
seemed so near to her and to her Charleston friends.

"I will call to-morrow," said Mr. Waite, as he left the
little girl at her own door. "And tell your father that
he had best not go on the streets unless he goes with
my brother or myself."

This last message made Sylvia very sober. She
came into the sitting-room holding her packages,
and found her mother and Mrs. Carleton busy with
their sewing, while her father was at his desk writing.
She repeated Mr. Waite's message, and her father
nodded silently.

Then Sylvia told them that the lockets and pictures
would be ready the following day. "And I have a doll
for Estralla," she concluded.

"Why not make the doll a fine dress and mantle?"
suggested Mrs. Carleton. "Come up to my room and I
will help you," and Sylvia agreed smilingly.

Mrs. Carleton had a roll of crimson silk in her work-
bag and before supper time the new doll was dressed
and ready for Estralla.

"This is for you, Estralla," Sylvia said, when
Estralla came up to her room, as she often did in the
late afternoon.

"Fer me, Missy! He, he, I knows w'en you's jokin'; but 'tis a fine lady doll," responded the little girl, wishing with all her heart that the beautiful doll in the gorgeous silken dress which Sylvia was holding toward her might really be hers.

"Take it, Estralla! It is for you. Truly it is," and Sylvia's tone was so serious that Estralla came slowly forward and took the doll.

For a moment the two little girls stood looking at each other in silence, Sylvia smiling, but Estralla with a surprised, half-anxious expression.

"Don't be afraid of it. Can't you have a doll of your own?" said Sylvia.

"Mebbe I can," replied Estralla, and then two big tears ran down her black cheeks.

"I'se got so much now, Missy Sylvia, dat I dunno as 'tis safe fer me to hev a doll," she whispered; but in a moment she was all smiles, and ran off to show her new treasure to her mother.

The pictures and the lockets proved all that Sylvia had hoped, and on New Year's day, when Grace came in for her daily visit, Sylvia gave her a small package.

"Please open it, Gracie!" she said, all eagerness to see her friend's delight.

Mr. Fulton had purchased a slender chain for each locket, and as Grace held up the pretty gift she exclaimed delightedly: "Oh, Sylvia! It is lovely, and I'll always wear it," and looked at the tiny picture of her friend with smiling satisfaction.

Sylvia had written a letter to Flora, and Grace promised to see that the locket and letter should reach her safely.

Every day Mr. Robert Waite or his brother escorted Mr. Fulton upon any errand of business to which he was obliged to attend. News had reached Charleston that a steamer with supplies and reinforcements for Major Anderson was on its way, and Mr. Robert Waite declared that the Confederates would never permit it to reach the fort.

Mrs. Carleton was very anxious. She had not received any message from her husband.

"If I could sail a boat I would go to Fort Sumter myself," she said one morning as she and Sylvia stood at a window overlooking the harbor.

"I can sail a boat," responded Sylvia.

Mrs. Carleton turned and looked at the little girl.

"If all this trouble ends in war, if the Confederates really dare fire upon the flag of the United States, I do not know how I can get any word from my husband," she said.

Sylvia thought that her friend's voice sounded as if she were about to cry, and the little girl slipped her

hand into Mrs. Carleton's. She wished there was something she could say to comfort her. Then she thought
quickly that there was something.

"I'll sail you over to the fort to see him whenever you
ask me to," she said impulsively.

"Dear child, I may have to ask you, but I hope not.
'Twould be a dangerous undertaking," she said, leaning over to kiss Sylvia's cheek.

That was the sixth of January, 1861, and on the
ninth a steamer, *The Star of the West*, with supplies and
reinforcements for Major Anderson, entered Charleston
harbor and was fired upon by a Confederate battery
concealed in the sand-hills at Sullivan's Island.

And now for many days the Fultons heard only dis-
couraging news. Everywhere there was great activity
among the Confederates. Mrs. Carleton became more
and more anxious for news of Captain Carleton, but she
did not remind Sylvia of her promise.

Grace and Sylvia were together a great deal, and
every morning Sylvia would run out to the front porch
to wave a good-bye to Grace on her way to school. Then
there was Estralla's lesson hour, her own studies, and
Mrs. Carleton was teaching her to crochet a silk purse
as a gift to Mr. Robert Waite, so that Sylvia did not
think very much about the soldiers at Fort Sumter.

"What do you think about starting for Boston with

us, Mrs. Carleton?" Mr. Fulton said one night just as
Sylvia was going up-stairs. "I really think the time has
come for me to take Sylvia and her mother to Boston,
and I am sure Captain Carleton would want you to go
with us."

"And Estralla and Aunt Connie will go, too; won't they,
Father?" said Sylvia, running back to her father's side.

"Yes, child. But I thought you were up-stairs,"
responded Mr. Fulton. "Do not speak of our leaving
Charleston to anyone. Remember. Not to Grace or
Estralla, until your mother or I give you permission."

Sylvia promised. It seemed to her the best of good
news that they would soon see Grandmother Fulton,
and she went happily off to bed thinking of all she
would have to tell her grandmother, and of the long letters she would write to Flora and Grace. "And when
summer comes they must both come and make me a
visit," she thought, little knowing that when summer
came no little southern girl would be allowed to visit a
Boston girl.

CHAPTER XX

"TWO LITTLE DARKY GIRLS"

"When will Mr. Lincoln be President?" Sylvia asked a few mornings after her father's announcement of his intention to return to Boston.

"He was inaugurated yesterday," replied her mother.

"Then can't Captain Carleton go north with us?" asked Sylvia, who had convinced herself that when Mr. Lincoln was in charge of the Government that all the troubles over Charleston's forts would end.

But Mrs. Fulton shook her head.

"Captain Carleton must stay and perhaps fight to defend the flag," she replied. "I wish we could leave at once, but we must stay as long as we can."

Sylvia listened soberly. She wondered what her mother would say if she knew off her promise to Mrs. Carleton to take a message to Fort Sumter if Mrs. Carleton should ask her to do so.

The warm days of early March made the southern city full of fragrance and beauty. Many flowers were in bloom, the hedges were green, and the air soft and warm. Sylvia and Grace often spoke of Flora, and wished that they could again visit the plantation.

Philip had brought Sylvia a letter from Flora, thanking her for the locket, and hoping that they would see each other again. Philip had not come into the house. He seemed much older to Sylvia than he did on her visit to the plantation in October. He said that Ralph was in the Confederate army. "I'd be a soldier if I was only a little older," he declared; and Sylvia did not even ask him about Dinkie, or the ponies. She wished that she could tell him that very soon she was going to Boston, but she knew that she must not; so she said good-bye, and Philip walked down the path, and waved his cap to her as he reached the gate.

It had been many weeks since the *Butterfly* had sailed about Charleston harbor. But the little boat was in the charge of an old negro who took good care of it. The negro knew Sylvia, and he knew that it was through her interest in Estralla that the little negro girl and her mother had been given their freedom. Now and then he appeared at Aunt Connie's kitchen, and one warm day toward the last of March, when Sylvia was wandering about the garden, she saw Uncle Peter going up the walk to the rear of the house.

"Oh, Uncle Peter! Wait!" she called and ran to ask him about the boat.

Uncle Peter had a great deal of news to tell. He said that unless Major Anderson and his soldiers left Fort Sumter at once that all the forts, and the new batteries built by the Confederates, would open fire upon Sumter and destroy it.

"I hears a good deal, Missy, 'deed I does," he declared, "but I doan' let on as I hears. Massa Linkum he's gwine to send a lot o' big ships down here 'fore long. Yas, indeed."

"I wish I could have a sail in the *Butterfly* again," said Sylvia, a little wistfully.

"Do you, Missy? Well, I reckons you can. I doan' believe anybody'd stop me a-givin' yo' a little sail 'roun' de harbor," said Uncle Peter. "I 'spec's Major Anderson is a-waitin' an' a-watchin' fer dem ships of Massa Linkum to come a-sailin' in," continued the old negro; for it was a time when the colored people were eager and hopeful for some news that might promise them their freedom.

Sylvia knew that Mrs. Carleton was worried and unhappy. It was known in Charleston that Fort Sumter was near the end of its food supplies, and that unless the Government at Washington sent reinforcements and provisions very soon by ships that the little garrison would be at the mercy of the Confederates, who were daily growing in strength.

As Sylvia left Uncle Peter and walked back to the house she was thinking of her promise to Mrs. Carleton.

"Perhaps she won't ask me. But if I could go and see Captain Carleton, and tell him that she was going to

Boston with us, and then bring her back a message, I know she'd be happier," thought the little girl. And she thought, too, of the pleasure it would be to once more sail the *Butterfly* to Fort Sumter.

She sat down on the porch steps, and a moment later Estralla appeared bringing a plate of freshly baked sugar cookies from Aunt Connie.

"Mammy says she made these 'special for you, Missy," declared Estralla smilingly.

"I'll go and thank her myself," said Sylvia, taking the plate, and offering one of the cookies to Estralla.

"Uncle Pete he say as de soldiers at Fort Sumter mus' be gettin' hungry," said the little colored girl.

"I wish you and I could take Captain Carleton some of these cookies," responded Sylvia.

"If you was black like I is we could go a-sailin' right off to de fort in plain daylight," said Estralla.

Sylvia sprang to her feet so quickly that she nearly upset the plate of cookies.

"Could we? Oh, Estralla, could we really?" she exclaimed.

Estralla looked at her little mistress with wondering eyes.

"Yas, course; nobody'd mind two leetle nigger gals. But you ain't black, Missy."

"But, Estralla, listen. I could be black. You could rub soot from the chimney all over my face and hands. And

I could pin my hair close on top of my bead and twist one of your mammy's handkerchiefs tight over it. Then nobody would know me." Sylvia had quite forgotten the fine cookies. She was holding Estralla by the arm, and talking very rapidly. Estralla was almost frightened at Sylvia's eagerness.

"Yas, Missy; but what for do you wanter go?" she asked.

"Oh, Estralla! If the men are hungry we could carry them something to eat. But most of all I want to see Captain Carleton, and get some message for his wife. She is so unhappy to go away without a word."

"Come 'long down in de garden," said Estralla, now as interested as Sylvia herself, "an' tells me more whar' nobody'll be hearin'," and the two little girls hurried off to a far corner of the pleasant garden.

"Uncl' Peter won' let us take the boat," Estralla objected as Sylvia told her how easy the plan would be; "an' how be you gwine to get all blacked up without folks knowin' it?"

But Sylvia had an answer for every objection.

"I'll come to your cabin and dress up there, and I will ask your mammy to give me some food for a poor man. Some cookies and a cake," she said. "We will start early to-morrow morning. And, Estralla, we will have to tell Uncle Peter, or he won't let us have the boat."

"Lan', Missy, I'll do jes' w'at yo' says. But I reckon Uncle Pete won' let us. W'at yo' mammy gwine to think w'en you ain't home to your dinner?" responded Estralla. But she was finally convinced that Missy Sylvia could carry out the plan, and agreed to have a large quantity of soot ready at her mother's cabin the next morning.

Sylvia was glad that she had eaten only one of the cookies. She carried the remainder to her room and then went to the kitchen.

"Will you make me a fine big cake, Aunt Connie?" she asked.

"Lan', course I will, chile! But, w'at you wan' it fer?" answered Aunt Connie, smiling down at the little girl whom she loved so dearly.

"It's a secret, Aunt Connie! I want to give it away, and I don't want to tell even my mother until—well," and Sylvia hesitated a moment, and then continued, "until next week. Then I will tell her, and you too."

"Dat's right, Missy. I'll make yo' de finest cake I knows how. Le's see! I'll put citron, an' raisins, an' currants in it. An' butter! Yas, thar'll be a fine lot o' things in dat cake!" and Aunt Connie rolled her eyes, and lifted her hands as if she could already taste its richness.

All that afternoon Sylvia could think of nothing but the proposed trip. She sat with Mrs. Carleton a little while before supper, and told her of what Uncle Peter had said: that ships from the north were on the way to the aid of Fort Sumter.

"Oh! I do wish I could send the news to Sumter. It would give them all courage," said Mrs. Carleton.

Sylvia was for a moment tempted to tell her friend that she would carry the message, but she kept silent, thinking to herself that here was another reason for her to carry out her plan.

"If you could send a message to Captain Carleton what would you say?" questioned Sylvia, and Mrs. Carleton smiled at Sylvia's serious voice.

"Why, if I could only let him know that I was safe and well and going to Boston with you, in case Sumter really is attacked; I know that is what he wants to hear."

Mrs. Carleton's smile vanished. Sylvia realized that this kind friend was troubled, and wished with all her heart that she could say: "To-morrow I will tell you all about Captain Carleton." But she knew that she must keep silent until she had carried out her plan.

Sylvia was the first one at the breakfast table the next morning, and was delighted when her mother said that she and Mrs. Carleton were invited to luncheon at the house of a friend.

"Aunt Connie and Estralla will take good care of you," Mrs. Fulton added, and Sylvia felt her face flush. But she made no reply, and soon hurried to the cabin where Estralla was waiting for her.

It was still early in the forenoon when two little

negro girls, one carrying a large package wrapped in a newspaper, appeared at the wharf where the *Butterfly* was moored. Uncle Peter was not to be seen. But he had just left the boat, whose sail had not even been lowered, and the two girls hurried on board. In a moment Sylvia had unfastened the rope, pushed the boat clear of the landing, and rudder in hand was steering the boat out toward the channel.

Two or three men in uniform watched the little "darkies," as they supposed both the girls to be, with amusement. Negro children were always playing about, and no attention was paid to them.

"My landy," whispered Estralla, "dat was jes' as easy. W'at Uncle Pete do w'en he fin's de boat gone?"

But it happened that Uncle Peter had been sent on an errand to a distant part of the town, and before he returned the *Butterfly* was well down the harbor.

Once or twice a guard-boat passed them closely enough to make sure that there were only two colored children in the boat, and they came up under the walls of Fort Sumter without a hindrance. The sentries at the fort had watched the little craft with anxious eyes, wondering if it could be bringing any message. But when the soldiers looked down at the two little negro girls they laughed, in spite of their disappointment. When Sylvia said that her name was Sylvia Fulton, and that she had come to see Captain

Carleton, a sentry exclaimed: "That girl has blacked her face. She is white."

But Captain Carleton could hardly believe that it was his little friend Sylvia. And he was eager to hear all that she could tell him. Estralla held the cake and cookies, which she had carefully wrapped in a newspaper, and the Captain seemed as much pleased with the paper as with the cake.

"You can write a letter to Mrs. Carleton and we will take it," suggested Sylvia, and then she told him Uncle Peter's news: that the President was sending ships to the aid of the fort.

"That is great news," said the Captain; "if it is only true we may keep the fort for the Union."

Within the hour of their arrival Sylvia and Estralla were on their way home. The Captain had praised and thanked Sylvia for the loyal friendship that had prompted her visit.

"Mrs. Carleton and I will always remember your courage," he said, as he handed her the letter.

"I am so glad I thought about it; but it was really Estralla. She said if I was black we could come," Sylvia had replied.

Then the boat swung clear and headed toward Charleston.

"I am not going to land at the big wharves," said Sylvia. "I am going to that wharf near Miss Patten's garden. And then we'll tell Uncle Peter where the *Butterfly* is."

It was early in the afternoon when Estralla appeared at the door of her mammy's kitchen.

"Whar on airth you been? An' whar's yo' missy?" demanded Aunt Connie. "Didn' I makes her a fine om'lit fer her dinner, an' it's ruinated."

"Missy wants a big pitcher of hot water," replied Estralla, dancing about just beyond Aunt Connie's reach.

"Missy Sylvia say to tell you we been carryin' de cake to her fr'en', an' she gwine to tell you, Mammy, explained Estralla when her mammy had finally grasped her firmly by the shoulders.

"W'y didn' yo' say dat firs' place? H'ar's de hot water," and Estralla hurried off to help Sylvia scrub off the sticky soot which had so well disguised her; and when Mrs. Fulton and Mrs. Carleton returned they found a very rosy-faced smiling little girl on the porch all ready to tell them of her trip to Fort Sumter, and to give Mrs. Carleton the longed-for news from her husband.

CHAPTER XXI

FORT SUMTER IS FIRED UPON

WHEN Sylvia's father heard of her sailing the *Butterfly* to Fort Sumter he was greatly troubled.

"If it should be discovered that my daughter had carried a message to Fort Sumter we would all be in danger; even the Waites would give us up," he declared. "What made you undertake such a thing, Sylvia?"

The little girl explained as well as she could her wish to get news of Captain Carleton for his wife, and said that she was sure no one knew that she was a white girl. But Mr. Fulton was anxious and uneasy, and Sylvia began to realize that her secret adventure might bring serious results to those she loved best.

"I told Captain Carleton what Uncle Peter said about ships coming to help Fort Sumter," she said, feeling almost sure that her father would think this the worst of all, but determined to make a full confession. She resolved that never again would she make plans without telling her mother and father, for she was most unhappy at her father's troubled look, and at his disapproval.

"What?" exclaimed Mr. Fulton. "Did you tell Captain Carleton that reinforcements were coming to the aid of Fort Sumter?"

"Oh, yes, I did, Father," sobbed Sylvia, who was now sure that she had told the very worst of her acts.

But to her surprise she heard her father say: "Thank heaven! That may influence Anderson to hold the fort until help arrives," and his arm was about his little daughter, and she looked up through her tears to hear him say:

"The news you carried to the fort is just what they wanted to know. And it may help to save the Union. It is worth while for us all to face personal danger if it proves that you were of service."

Sylvia did not quite understand why Uncle Peter's news should be so important, but her father explained to her that Major Anderson would now feel sure of help, and that his men would have courage to bear hardship and hunger if need be until the ships arrived.

"And you forgive me for going?" Sylvia pleaded.

"My dear child! I am glad and proud that you could carry such a message to brave soldiers," her father replied, "but do not mention it to anyone. I must hasten my arrangements to leave Charleston. General Beauregard may fire upon Fort Sumter at any day, and I am of no use here."

Sylvia drew a long breath of relief. That her father should really praise her for what she had feared might prove a very serious mistake made the little girl happy although it did not change her resolve never again to make adventurous plans without the approval of her mother or father. She realized that, although she had carried a valuable message, she had also endangered her father's safety if her visit to the fort was discovered, as every southerner would believe that Mr. Fulton had made the plan to be of aid to the United States.

The little household now began its preparations to start north as soon as possible, and Sylvia was eager for the time to come that would see them safely on their way to their northern home. Grace Waite and her mother had gone into the country, and Sylvia did not know if she would see her friend again.

The morning of April 11, 1861, dawned brightly over the harbor of Charleston, whose waters were covered with white sails putting hastily to sea. Guard-boats were plying constantly between the harbor and the islands. It was rumored about the town that before sunset the Confederate batteries would open fire upon Fort Sumter.

Mr. Fulton's preparations to leave Charleston were completed, and if nothing prevented they would start for Boston on April 14th. On the eleventh, however, Mrs. Carleton hardly left the window from which she could look out over the harbor toward Fort Sumter. At any

"IT MAY HELP TO SAVE THE UNION"

moment it might be attacked, and she knew that such an attack meant the beginning of a terrible civil war.

Sylvia wandered about the house and garden with Estralla, telling the little colored girl of the home in Boston which she soon hoped to see.

The hours passed, and the streets of Charleston grew strangely quiet. At sunset everything was calm, and no sound of guns disturbed the peace of the April evening, and Sylvia went to bed at the usual hour, not thinking that she would be wakened by the roar of cannon. The older members of the family sat up until after midnight. The sea was calm, and the night still under the bright starlight. At last they decided to retire, but there was little sleep for them that night.

At half-past four the next morning the sound of guns from Fort Johnson broke upon the stillness. It was the signal to the Confederate batteries to open fire.

Hardly had the echo of the opening gun died upon the air when every Confederate fort and battery opened fire upon Sumter, until the fort was "surrounded by a circle of fire."

The Fulton household dressed hurriedly and from the windows looked over the harbor at the flashing lights and bursts of flame. Sylvia stood close beside Mrs. Carleton, and they were all silent.

Aunt Connie brought up hot coffee and a tray of food, but none of them cared to eat. Mr. Fulton waited anxiously for the sound of answering guns from Fort

Sumter. But not until seven o'clock that morning did Fort Sumter open its fire.

"War has begun," said Mr. Fulton gravely, turning away from the window.

"Will the President's ships come soon, Father?" asked Sylvia.

"We must hope so," he answered; "and now there is no time for us to lose. We must start at once."

"Bres' de Lord!" said Aunt Connie, who was standing near the door, and as Mr. Fulton spoke she hurried off to her cabin to make her final preparations for the long journey.

Mrs. Fulton hastened to pack up the few things they would take with them, and Sylvia helped Mrs. Carleton pack. Early in the forenoon they were ready. Mr. Robert Waite's carriage was at the door, with Mr. Waite, who had come to escort them on the first stage of their journey.

"I wish I could say good-bye to Grace," said Sylvia as she went down the steps of the porch. She was all ready to enter the carriage when she heard her name called: "Sylvia! Sylvia!" and Grace came flying up the path.

"Grace! Grace!" responded Sylvia, and for a moment the two little girls, "Yankee" and southern girl, clung closely together, while the noise of the echoing guns from the forts boomed over the harbor.

"We will always be friends, won't we, Sylvia?" said Grace; and Sylvia responded "Always." Then with one more good-bye kiss Grace turned and ran back to Mammy Esther. She had persuaded her mother to bring her to Charleston that she might bid Sylvia good-bye, and now they would hasten back to the country, for Charleston might be attacked by United States ships of war, and was no longer a place of safety.

The Fultons now entered the carriage. Aunt Connie and Estralla were the only members of the party who were smiling and happy. To Estralla it was the most wonderful day of her life. She was free. And with her mammy and her Missy Sylvia she was starting for a world where little colored girls could go to school, just as white children did, and never be bought or sold. She looked at Sylvia with adoring eyes.

"What are you thinking of, Estralla?" asked Sylvia.

Estralla leaned close to her "true fr'en'" and whispered: "I was a-t'inkin' 'bout my breakin' of de pitcher, an' a-spillin' de hot water, Missy Sylvia. You took my part den, Missy, an' you'se allers taken my part. My mammy say she bress de Lord dat you came to Charleston."

Sylvia smiled back at the little colored girl. For a moment she forgot the booming of the distant guns, and remembered only her friends and the happy days she had spent in her southern home.